Darrell's Walk to Freedom

"13 Years A Slave"

by

Jean Simester

Acknowledgements

For all the hard work of Chief Superintendent Paul Griffiths and Operation Imperial did in bringing to trial the men who did what they did to Darrell. In the end only one of the two went to prison which was for four and a half years, which wasn't really what I wanted but it was the result everyone wanted.
Most of the royalties of this book will go to Anti-Slavery and Victim Support.
Also a very kind thank you to everyone who contributed to the book.

Introduction

This book has been put together by Darrell, my husband Tony and I. There are statements from his brother and others who wanted to contribute.
With the help and support from family and friends, we have brought together our search for our son/brother, over 13 very hard years.
How we found him, the struggle to get help, how we were treated by police, doctors, social services etc
The trial and the conviction of his captor.
Modern Day Slavery - how it still goes on, in this day and age.

Dedication

I would like to thank the following as without them, I honestly do think that I would never have found our son.

Firstly, my husband Tony and our youngest, Duncan, who, like us, NEVER GAVE UP.

Vern Wright, Gregg Lane, Frazer Kinny, Pamela Gurney, Kat Foy, Jan Sullivan, Clare Hutchinson, Fiona Willetts & Liz Finn, Paul Lofthouse & Alex Wharton, Paul Cole, Paul Griffiths and the Operation Imperial team at Gwent Police.

Chapter 1

A Little About Darrell

First of all I would like to say a little about our son Darrell. He was born on 4th October 1969. He was a healthy baby weighing 8lbs 3ozs. He had dark hair and blue eyes. His progress was fantastic, very forward in all aspects, until he was nine months old. Out of the blue, this happened!

He was sat on my lap one day, when all of a sudden he fell backwards, limp and lifeless. Instinct kicked in, I puffed short puffs of my breath into his tiny body. My mother-in-law was just about to leave when it happened. Thankfully within a short time Darrell came to, as if nothing had happened. My mom-in-law went to telephone Tony at work, to ask him to come home. Our doctor was called also, he came straight away, Darrell was given an injection and we were told to take him to Worcester Hospital.

On the first two occasions of this happening to Darrell we had to take him to hospital. We were told it was 'a high temperature'.

We had to take him to Powick Hospital for E.E.G. Tony freaked the first time he witnessed Darrell having a turn.

Doctors told us this was happening because he was teething and it was his body's way of coping, they said it was convulsions that he was having that was causing the trouble. Darrell was put on medication until he was at primary school, he was 5 years old. By now his convulsions had ceased.

Darrell was always in a mainstream school but he was always bottom grade classes. He was never any trouble, he was quiet and polite. He went to Franche First and Middle Schools then higher education at Harry Cheshire Secondary Modern. When he left school he hadn't achieved any high levels in G.C.S.E. At the time of leaving school, Y.T.S was a way of getting a job and that was what he did. He always had dirty menial jobs, cleaning, grafting, menial jobs, never a good clean employment.

As time went by and Darrell grew up, he was always willing to please and help people, nothing wrong with that, as all our children are the same. Sometimes, this was taken advantage of, by so-called 'friends'. He loved helping his dad run a boys football team, he would be 'bucket man' or linesman or even other little jobs, like putting nets up.

Around the age of 21 he announced he had met a girl. Darrell began dressing smartly and made more of an effort with his appearance. Unfortunately however, she cheated on Darrell, and he was heartbroken. It broke his heart and we don't think he had another proper girlfriend after.

He liked to go for a drink as he got older and this is where, in my honest opinion, it all started to go wrong. Darrell got in with a family who preyed on his vulnerability. He was after all, old enough to choose his friends. He told us he was going to move in with some men he worked with, sharing a flat. This didn't last long, as he hadn't kept up with his share of the rent, etc, so he went to live with this family he had befriended. He used to pop in and visit us, whenever he wished.

In 1997, Tony had a nasty accident at work, falling into an inspection pit. He sustained a compound fracture of the right femur. I was working 40 hours a week and while Tony was in hospital I was literally commuting from home to work, to the hospital and home to bed. Darrell, along with the other 3 children, visited him in hospital. Darrell looked very pale and fainted when he saw his dad.

We would see Darrell now and again and he would say how this family made him take their children to school before he could go to bed after a nightshift at work. (We were told after the court case, that they had made him sleep on a bed in their shed. Also they would take him to the A.T.M on a Friday, make him draw his wages out and give him £20 for pocket money. We did not know this at the time, it only came out after the court case.

In the latter part of November 1997, we moved house to live in a mobile home, Darrell would come and visit us. Around the June or July of 1998, I became aware he was living rough and begging for money. We searched for him and couldn't find him. I would go to the park late at night to see if he was on a bench. We never saw him until October 1998, when Duncan spotted him walking around with a shopping trolley. He smelt and was filthy dirty and clearly living rough. He told Duncan this 'family' had told him to go and siphon diesel from lorries and if he didn't go back with some, he would be beaten up.

We had him live with us. Duncan provided clothes, shoes etc, for him. He told us he was made to steal diesel and drive cars. I asked, "How could you drive their car, you never had lessons?" He said 'they' made him do things regardless and because he was afraid of what they might do to him, he did as he was told.

Darrell made me swear I would not tell the 'family' he was living with us. He was clearly terrified of them. We encouraged him to look for a job and find somewhere to live and be independent. I helped him with both putting a deposit on a flat, I would do his washing, take him shopping. I explained that he 'must' pay his rent etc before spending any money, we provided him with bedding, TV and other items to help.

Within a short time, I had a phone call from the landlord saying Darrell hadn't been paying rent and the 'family' had been hanging around and asked Darrell to move back in with them, which he did. Darrell would visit us once a week, with his washing. On one occasion he had a split nose and other black eyes. He said he was attacked in the subway. I didn't believe him. At the start of 2000, nothing had changed, Darrell visited regularly. We constantly asked him to move back home. He plodded on with his job, as per normal.

Chapter 2

The Nightmare Begins

It was while he was with this family that Darrell went on holiday and left (because all they took him away for was to look after their children).

The date that will always stick in my mind is: Friday 11th August, 2000. Tony was at work, when Darrell came to visit. He told me he was going on holiday to Porthcawl and said, "We are going tomorrow for a week. I will come and see you next Saturday or Sunday when we are back."

Little did I know that, that was to be the last time I would see him for nearly 13 years.

The search begins for Darrell

The following weekend, we were expecting Darrell to visit us, of course it never happened but what followed was surreal.

On Sunday 19th August, 2000, I was at home on my own, Tony was at work, when I heard a knock at the door. I answered to see an unkempt woman standing there. She explained that she had been to Porthcawl also and they had come back without Darrell. There had been a fight and Darrell just went off. No clothes or money. They had apparently looked for him but could not find him. They had been to the police and reported Darrell as 'missing'.

This was the beginning of our nightmare. I contacted Kidderminster Police Station and told them what I had been told. An officer arrives to take details. Over the following days we make contact with the police, from Wales, who say they had been unable to trace him and they wanted us to do a television appeal, to which we agreed. Before this could get set up, an officer from Wales telephoned me to say that two officers on patrol had found Darrell, sleeping rough; they asked him if he is ok and if he needed to contact anyone. It appears Darrell said he was ok and they left it at that.

If only they had chatted with him? Maybe they could have taken him to the local police station and called us? These questions I asked. As he was an adult they said that was all they could do! This answer would be given to us many times, in our search for Darrell.

Days passed by and then out of the blue I received a phone call to my mobile.

It was Darrell. He said he was with two men, who called themselves 'Johnny and Tommy Docherty'. They had Irish accents and I could not understand them so I gave the mobile to Tony. They told him that they will look after Darrell and give him work. They also said we could contact him or them on a mobile number. (The number they were using).

Both Tony and I were not happy but Darrell was adamant that he would go to work with them. There was a long telephone conversation between Tony, Darrell and these two men before eventually it was decided Darrell wanted to give it a try down in Wales as he been disillusioned with being beaten up back in Kidderminster. Tony asked about keeping in touch regularly and Darrell said he would. Tony also asked about where he would be living, an address, but the men told him they travelled all over and for that reason they could not give an address.

Finally, Tony asked Darrell if he was sure he was ok and did he want to come home, he said no he wanted to give it a go. We had to accept he was going to be living and working in Wales. We asked him to phone us regularly and let us know how he was.

The telephone calls were very random, never for birthdays, Christmas, Mother's Day, Father's Day etc. We would phone and ask to speak with Darrell. Sometimes we could talk to him, other times we were told he was working for someone else.

January 2001, Zoe gives birth to Jordan, Darrell's nephew. Next time he calls I ask him for his address once again, so that we can send him photographs BUT he says, "I can't".

As time went on and the calls were very random, we kept phoning the police. Someone would visit; we would recall everything that had happened, how we NOW felt that Darrell was being held against his will. As EVERYTIME we spoke to him, you could hear someone in the background telling him what to say.

One time, when he phoned us, (12th February, 2006), he told us he was married to a lady named Mary and had a little girl named Lisa who was two years old and there was another baby on the way!!! Not in any of his earlier calls had he mentioned a wife or child.

Another phone call, he told me he was living in Ireland. The things Darrell was now coming out with were putting more and more suspicions in our mind. We were convinced he was being held against his will.

Our minds were working overtime, wondering where he was, was he healthy? Was he happy?

All this time I am doing everything I can think of to try and find him. On the internet searching his name, leaving messages on any 'Missing' sites I could find. I contacted numerous associations for missing people. E-mailing different police, here and in Ireland... Again, I had to recall everything over and over. It was so upsetting every time I had to do it.

Whenever Darrell telephoned us it would break my heart. "Hello Mom, it's me Darrell." I asked for an address, to send cards and photos but was always told, "I CANT tell you".

I text, I phone the number most times but no reply. I have the number in my mobile and try it randomly, hoping to speak to him. Three times I left an answer message on the number. First time was April 2005 to give him the bad news about his favourite cousin Mark, who had been tragically killed while riding his motorbike, and we wanted him home for the funeral. Second time was November 2007, his Auntie Pam had passed away after her battle with breast cancer, and thirdly his Uncle Mick (Mark's Dad) also lost his life to cancer.

We knew Darrell would have wanted to pay his respects but 'THEY' obviously never passed on my messages.

September 2006, Zoe has another boy, Baylee, yet another nephew he hasn't been able to see....

We still had random calls but now the phone number was either 'withheld' or 'unknown', so now we have no way of getting in touch. I still try the number in my phone, with the hope that someone will answer and I could get a message to Darrell.

We go out for the day and I am always looking at workmen, hoping to see him. I'm searching faces in the crowds, looking at the homeless people, tramps; the unknown was sometimes unbearable. I couldn't stand to celebrate Christmas, as our family was not complete.

I am forever contacting the police, please help? But no! They were not interested...

Our last contact with Darrell was while we were in Spain for Christmas, for a holiday with Duncan and his family. We were sat outside, enjoying the sun. 24th December, 2008. The mobile rings - the number is 'withheld'. I answer, it's Darrell.

"Hi Mom, it's me Darrell." Tony and Duncan are talking to me saying "Get his number and we will phone him back because of charges while we are abroad". Voices are in the background again, Darrell says he can't give the number but will phone us in the New Year. He says "bye" and that was the last time I spoke with him, until we found him, on Thursday 28th February, 2013.

We have to carry on, as normal as we can, we have other children and we have grandchildren - two of which Darrell hadn't seen. To some people, they didn't know the pain we were going through, they simply thought we were ok. I am constantly reporting Darrell as a 'Missing Person' but I am sure they think we are paranoid, worrying over him.

Police were given the mobile number we had for Darrell, and they came back with "We can't trace it"! The mobile number was given to them in September 2007. They said it's "No longer recognised and at the time of a call at 13.30 today was not accepting calls". (This is taken from their email.) I'm repeatedly reporting Darrell 'Missing'. WHY won't someone LISTEN?

Each year after our last call in December 2008 it gets worse. Where is he? Is he ok?

I need to find him before we die.

January 2009:

We wait for Darrell to telephone us, as he said he would. No telephone calls, what is going on?

Why does he not telephone?

It's been too long, since the last telephone call 24/12/2008.

I am now getting very worried. I get in touch with the police, YET again!

I am constantly asking for help to find him.

I am worried to death, I've not heard from him. Tony is telling me to stop searching, he was convinced that Darrell was dead BUT I was not going to give up on my son. He wouldn't not call me, if he was able to.

THEY are stopping Darrell being in contact with us!

I WILL NEVER GIVE UP...

Police, come and go, take statement after statement. I am getting very angry and nasty with them. WHY do they not take us seriously?

I search and search until I FIND him. I will try anything to see him again, no matter how long it takes.

Chapter 3

Facebook
This is where it all comes together...

In 2012, I joined a group on Facebook, 'Kidderminster Friends, Past, Present & Future' (KFPP&F). It's just a site for people to chat about all sorts of topics.

Summer is here, I'm sat in the garden using the laptop, and still searching... I'm thinking of more ways to find Darrell... I'll post his photograph on KFPP&F... perhaps someone might know where he is... anything is worth a go...

"Can You Help? Do You Know My Son?"

A message pops up from a chap named Vern Wright, who says he knew Darrell from school... "I can start a 'Missing Darrell Simester page. We can add friends and family and get everyone to do the same. Let's get it out there and find Darrell."

I was stunned that someone was willing to put themselves out to help us.

The page was created on 22nd June, 2012. (Ironic, as 22nd June was his cousin Mark's birthday.) Vern adds me with all his family and friends on Facebook... I add my family and friends... On June the 25th we have 3,729 members helping us...

I post on the page... Thankyou Vern for your help, it's restored my faith in human kindness...

VERN: You're most welcome Jean, I'm sure with the help of Kidderminster Friends and beyond we can scan the world for him.

ME: Let's hope so!

This is what I wrote on 'Missing Darrell Simester'

Hi, Friends,

I am Darrell's mom, Jean, if you need to ask me anything about him please e-mail me at flowersbyj@hotmail.co.uk. Darrell went on holiday to Wales on 12th August 2000 and the last time we spoke with him was Xmas Eve 2008, he had been in Cork Ireland. He had been working on the roads with 2 Irishmen, Johnny and Tom Docherty. Whenever we have spoken to Darrell it's as though someone is telling him what or what not he can say to us... he would never give us an address and he did give us a mobile number once and then next time told us he had lost it. I still have 3 numbers which we used to be able to phone and messages would be passed on... the police don't want to know as they say "No news is good news, if he was dead we would contact you"!!! Missing People and the Salvation Army have not been able to find him... hopefully, someone might have seen him. We live in hope. We could understand if we had done something to have made him go but we have since found out that the couple he went on holiday with, the bloke beat Darrell up and off Darrell went.... sorry for going on, a broken-hearted mom.

I update with the following...

Just a few more details. Darrell went to Franche First and Middle School and then to Harry Cheshire... we lived on Franche Estate until 1989 when we moved into the Unity Pub, where we lived for 2 years then we lived on Worcester road. Kidderminster... Darrell lived with us until he was 28. Darrell is a very vulnerable person and would be easily led... he is about 5 foot 8 inches and slight build dark brown hair blue eyes...If I think of anything else I will update this post. Thanks everyone for your help so far, I am amazed. Jean.

26th June 6,307 members... Wow!

27th June Vern posts on the site...

A massive thankyou to all of you kind-hearted people for joining in and spreading the group for Darrell's family. We hope and pray that he is found soon, keep on adding your friends to the list, the more people that know the better and please tag yourselves in Darrell's photo that enables it to be seen far and wide. We can't thank you enough for your support. Vern.

28th June 8,088... people are added from as far as Australia, Austria, Turkey, Germany, New Zealand, Canada and Ireland. We have thousands and thousands join. I leave posts for Darrell 'Just in case'!

Zoe, (Darrell's sister), is getting married in August 2012 and she wants him there, so we keep pushing, hoping we can find him for her BIG day.

By now we have 9,500 people on the Facebook 'Missing Darrell Simester' page.

A police officer emails me saying he wants to help as much as he can; he's not with our local police force. He says we have been treated abysmally. He tells me he is going to put me in contact with an Inspector Superintendent for 'Missing People', the guy has had a recommendation from the Queen for all his hard work. He's their guru on Missing People.

Correspondence and finally a telephone call... He listens to my story THEN has the nerve to say "Darrell is a Missing Contact"! I tell him in no uncertain terms "Darrell is my son NOT a Missing Contact, how dare he tell anyone that their flesh and blood is a 'Contact'?" I swear if EVER I come face to face with this so called 'Guru', I will swing for him. I hate him with a vengeance. How tactless and stupid is he?

July 15th 2012 2.46 p.m. I post on Missing Darrell Simester...

Well my lovely son, your baby sister is getting married on 4th August, so I'm praying you will phone me, your worried mom, and let me know you are ok and could come home for the day... really need to know you are ok and could come home for the day... really need to know you are alive and well and IF some shithole of a person is holding you against your wishes you can escape and phone us to come and get you... love you so much and miss you like crazy x x x

A private investigator gets in touch with me and asks for the mobile numbers we have for Darrell. I tell him the police have said they cannot trace it but he says, "Please let me have it".

Within 5 minutes he telephones me and says, "It's attached to a paving company in Rumney, Wales."

How come the 'Police' couldn't find out this????

Brendan, Darrell's brother, goes onto the computer and researches 'Rumney Paving Company'. He finds that they have a 'sister' company in Ireland and another in Gloucestershire. It all seems to be coming together. We can see a glimmer of hope.

Friday 20th July 2012 5.58 p.m. My post on Missing Darrell Simester.

Can you believe it, the police have e-mailed me to say that they are not treating Darrell as a 'Missing Person' just a 'Missing Contact'...?

I am so fuming mad there is steam coming out of my ears... what a fucking waste of space the police are.

Brendan and Duncan arrange to go to Rumney on 21st July 2012, (Zoe's hen night). The P.I telephones Duncan and tells him to go to the local police station and explain why they are there, as the area is known for travellers... to be careful as the local police won't go near.

Duncan looks online and was astonished by what he read. He tells me, "We will find him, Mom, no matter how long it takes."

The boys go off on the Saturday morning to Cardiff. We get a telephone call at lunchtime. They have been to the police station and they won't even let the lads talk in private. They feel intimidated outside the local pub and we tell them to not go in and come home. They say they are going into the betting shop next door with a photo of Darrell. Someone in there says they have seen Darrell a couple of weeks before. They phone again with this news and its tears all round... (It turns out Darrell had NEVER been in the betting shop.)

When the lads get back home and tell me how badly they had been treated at the police station, I am livid. I'm on the internet searching for who is in charge.

The following weekend Tony and I go down to Cardiff. This time on the Sunday. We went into the pub and many others, showing Darrell's photo. No one had seen him or knew him. We are told that there were two traveller sites. We drove to Shirenewton and Roverway. We went in one and spoke to the two managers who oversee both camps. They didn't know him.

By now I have found out who is in charge at the Rumney police station and I e-mail her. Her reply was not really friendly, no dear or hello, just Jean. I reply that I don't like the way she starts her emails. She apologises and promises to call me, which she did. I explain I am not happy with the way the lads had been treated at her station. I tell her why they went down to Rumney. How Darrell was missing and we believed he was in the area. I get the promise of help but she is going on annual leave and tells me she is putting her deputy in charge, also a liaison officer with the traveller community, and another woman for missing people.

Anyway, Welsh Police are as useless as our police. They don't let me know what they are doing to help with looking for Darrell. They ignore my e-mails. We eventually find out that they (South Wales Police) have been in contact with our police force and were told that Darrell was a 'Missing Contact', so literally they have been told not to search for him....

Zoe's wedding day arrives and NO big brother... she has a wonderful day and Darrell was mentioned by Tony in his speech... a little compromise was, we surprised her with a wedding horse and carriage, her dream transport when she was younger....

Chapter 4

Darrell's Birthday

October 4th 2012, Darrell's birthday. Tony has printed off some posters; he's off to Cardiff to give them out. He stuck them to lampposts and gave them to shopkeepers. He gets home drained and emotional. Some people were willing to help, others didn't want to know. He says he will go back...

The officer that had contacted me through Facebook's 'Missing Darrell Simester' page phones me, to ask if he could arrange for an officer to visit us and arrange for someone to take a 'Statement'. This gets arranged for November 28th, 2012.

All through this I am still searching the internet. I am writing emails to police forces in Ireland, Councillors in Wales, Salvation Army, Missing People, No one gives any answers. Posting on every site I could. Up most nights, just searching and hoping!

I believed we would find him! One day.

The interview at home that was arranged for 28th November was done! Duncan and Zoe came straight from work to sit with us. At 5 p.m. the officer from Kidderminster police station came. 4 hours we sat, answering some of the most stupid questions. We are told that this statement would be going to the officer in charge and then to someone who had not been involved in this case, to give an unbiased result as to whether Darrell was in fact a 'Missing Person' OR a 'Missing Contact'. He tells us he will take this statement away and get it typed up for us to read and sign. Days later a lady officer comes with the statement, I am annoyed as soon as I start to read it, they haven't even spelt Darrell's name correctly. I've had enough: the police are an utter waste of time. I sit and correct every single mistake in the statement, it even said that Darrell had got married while he had been on holiday, do they not listen to what they are told? I know they DON'T. A few more days pass by and the statement is eventually as good as it gets and we will have a decision before Christmas. (So we are told.)

We asked the officer who did the interview to give a letter to the officer in charge, that we had written, it read...

Dear Sir,

As the parents of Darrell Lee Simester, who was born on 4th October 1969, we would like you to understand, what it is like not to have heard from your son in 4 years.

You will now be aware of our situation but when Darrell came to see his mom, on Friday evening 11th August of 2000, to tell her he was going on holiday the next day with some friends, neither of us realised that that would be the last we ever saw of him.

He was after all 30 years old but we did not know at the time, that the family he was going with were continually beating him up. Whilst on holiday, he was beaten up again and he decided that he had had enough.

His mom has contacted several companies over the last 12 years to try and locate him, without success. Police Forces, Welsh, West Mercia and Irish, The Salvation Army, Missing Person and Missing People have all said they would help but no one ever has. So many different officers have been to our house and my wife has had to go through bitter memories telling these different officers the story.

An Inspector Crawley came here once and said to my wife, "Well good news is no news; if he were dead you would be told". How insensitive is that?

My wife has asked me to write to you because some of the things that have been said and promises made have hurt my wife. I ask you, do you think officers should say the quote from the previous paragraph?

Personally I believe we have been let down by the police. I understand you have your hands tied with the protection rubbish but in this situation, we have continually told police and anyone who would listen that we believe Darrell must be held against his will, or he is scared to get in touch because of repercussions. Of course I have no proof of that but why would he not have telephoned home, he just wouldn't do that to his mom.

Our conversation with the officer, last Wednesday 28th November was very good. He asked lots of personal questions, which we didn't mind answering and he was here for about 4 hours, 5 pm until 9 pm, which came to an abrupt end when he was summoned to help with a break-in, in Hagley. I was just thinking, this is the first time someone has called and not had to dash off, when he had his call, just proving to me the police are understaffed and people like my wife and I are just a waste of police time.

Before leaving the officer asked me, "Do you think your son is vulnerable?" I told him how I couldn't give an honest answer to that question, when I haven't seen my son in 12 years. He was vulnerable when I last knew of him, easily led by others more confident than himself. Scared of his own shadow, I never saw him stand up for himself, in 30 years though we all grow up and who knows how our son is now. As far as I know he has been living or been friends with the travelling community, how can I say how he would be now?

He may even be a hard case now but one thing I am 100% certain of is, there is no way that he would not phone his mom.

If the police can contact him and tell him he has to phone home, he will. I don't think that will happen though because I don't think you will contact him. I am ill but I will not give up. My last lead took us to Rumney in South Wales, I went and put posters up but nothing has happened from that. However when the weather improves in the spring, I will go back to Rumney in Cardiff and stay for as long as it takes to find our son. It is killing both his mom and me; I will not rest until I find him.

If you know of his whereabouts, you could tell me, Darrell would not mind, of that I am certain. He could be married now, I don't know but I am desperate to contact our son, please help us.

Yours faithfully
Jean & Tony Simester

Chapter 5

Missing Adults & Children in the UK

2012 / 2013

Missing Adults and Children in the UK are now on 'Missing Darrell Simester', they are encouraging me to keep up the search, give offers of ideas, they put Darrell's picture out regularly on their website, Twitter account and also their Facebook page. A lady (Pamela Gurney) contacts me through Darrell's page and asks me a few questions. Does he like horses? I tell her he liked horse racing and all animals. She tells me that she can see Darrell working with horses and he's in Sligo - Ireland. Well as we had been told by Darrell, in one of his phone calls that he was in Ireland, it seemed possible! After this news, it's arranged for me to do a 'LIVE' appeal on Ocean FM Radio on Monday 3rd December 2012. I was petrified of doing it, but needs must...

I could not eat, all over the weekend, with fear of doing this 'live appeal'. I announce on Darrell's page what I am about to do. Lots of people let me know they wish me luck and hope that something positive comes out of it. On the morning of the appeal I am in bits, shaking with nerves... I did the appeal, describing Darrell as best I could. Obviously, as he was never in Ireland, we had no response. Never mind, it was an experience I would not like to do again...

We don't hear from the police. No report for us to see or read. I knew not to hold my breath. Tossers the lot of them!

Christmas Eve 2012. My message for Darrell.

My Dearest Darrell, it's 4 years today that I last heard your voice... I'm wishing you a Very Merry Christmas, wherever you are. Love and miss you so much. I really need to know you are alive and well, can't take much more of this not knowing. Please God can someone find my boy... love you Darrell... Mom x x x

New Year's Eve. My message...

Well Darrell, another year is coming to an end; let's hope 2013 will be the year we find you. Happy New Year Son. Love and miss you x x x

January 3rd 2013. It's on the news that slaves have been released from Todbury Farm in Gloucester. I email the D.C.I in charge, asking if Darrell is one of them. No Luck! He's not one of the slaves released...

January 4th 2013 7.56 p.m. I write on Missing Darrell Simester.

Been thinking of everything I want to do to find you, newspapers, radio stations, more posters etc; we will go back to Rumney as your Dad has the gut feeling that's where you are.... Lots of people know you as 'Darrell', some called you 'Simmo' or 'Daz', hopefully someone might recognise one of your names...

It's really hard trying to think of things to do and places to look, we are STILL awaiting an answer from the 4 hour statement we made to police as to see if they think you are a 'Missing Person' or a 'Missing Contact'.... how they can say to a PARENT your son is a missing contact? I just can't understand AND I will NEVER accept this. He's my first born child and he's missing. Please friends of Missing Darrell Simester, keep adding your contacts and keep searching faces and hopefully one of you will see his face and make my dream come true. Thanks to you all...

Pamela Gurney, who had said about Darrell being with horses and in Sligo sends me an e-mail address for the editor of a Welsh Newspaper. I write my email to him, explaining we need a story about Darrell being missing... I get a reply on January 31st, 2013.

16th February, 2013... I write on Missing Darrell Simester.

Well, last night I spoke with someone from the Welsh newspaper, they ARE going to do a story for us. Will keep you all posted, as I think you all deserve to know what is happening... On that note, I still have not had a reply form the police from the statement that was taken on 28th November 2012... Thanks Folks x x x

I'm now in contact with the Welsh Echo, emails back and forth with as much details as we can give, at last we can get our story out there.

25th February, 2013 11.48 a.m. 'Missing Darrell Simester'...

Our appeal for Darrell is in today's Wales Online newspaper... just in case any of you are interested. Family and friends copy our appeal and put on their pages. We need as many people to read this...

We receive a paper copy in the post, the next day.

26th February, 2013. It's over 24 hours and we haven't had any response from the newspaper appeal.

We are watching the television, when my mobile rings. I take myself off into the kitchen to answer it. A woman's voice asks for me! She tells me, "I'm 95% certain I know where your son is". (At this point I can't believe what I am hearing.) "I've spoken to him, he said his name was Daz and I replied, that's a funny name, what's your real name, he replied it's Darrell, he seems ok." (All this news is making me tearful.) "I will give you directions where to find him." She proceeded to give me directions, (which I'm trying to write down with tears streaming down my face)'. I ask for her name. "I can't give it, just in case. I saw your appeal in the paper and I had to call you." I thanked her for calling and said goodbye.

I've gone into Tony, crying my eyes out, can't talk. I eventually tell him what's happened. We phone Brendan, Duncan and Zoe. Zoe is worried it may be a hoax but we must go. Tony told Duncan, "We are going down to Cardiff tonight"

Duncan: Dad you can't go tonight, I will drive you down Thursday.

Tony: We will go tomorrow.

Duncan: Dad, you are not going on your own, I have commitments tomorrow, which I can't get out of, one more day won't hurt.

Fingers crossed!

We arrange to go on the morning of Thursday 28th February, 2013. We only tell a handful of people what we are going to do.

Thursday can't come soon enough.....

Chapter 6

Our Journey to Peterstone

I post on my own Facebook page at 8.09 a.m. Today, this could be The Greatest Day of our lives... Take That.

Duncan arrives as promised and off we go, with the directions on a bit of paper. We chat about what Darrell may look like, tattoos, beard, piercings, kids, wife etc. Getting ever nearer to where the directions are for, we are full of apprehension. Are we going to find him at last?

Driving down the road we have been given, Duncan suddenly stops and reverses on to a driveway.

Tony: What are you stopping for?

Duncan: I'm going to ask directions, won't be a min.

Off he goes across the road, we watch him walk through the gates, he's talking to someone, and we can't see who. Duncan's coming back to the car. He gives us the thumbs up! We don't know what he means. On getting back into the car he tells us, "It's Darrell, he's a mess, didn't recognise me. I told him, 'I've got your mom and dad in the car, do you want to come and see them?' He asked how I knew you and I told him, "I'm your brother, Duncan. He also said 'you will have to come back later when I lock the gates, I can speak to you then. I've got to get on with my work, THEY will be watching me."

Duncan tells me to phone the police, just in case there is any trouble.

I call the police; explain in a rushed panicked voice what we wanted them to do. The lady, who was on the other end of the phone, tells me that we have got through to the wrong area. She took my name and mobile number and said "someone will phone you back". We sit in the car opposite where Darrell is. We cannot see him. The police call back asking questions, 'what colour car are you in? etc etc'; I'm getting really mad by now and I am shouting that 'this is not a hoax, I want my son out of there'. We are told to wait in the car until officers arrive.

Duncan suggests we drive just up the road and he would hang around by the farm. Tony and I sit and wait what seemed to be ages. We can see Duncan walking up the road to us. When he gets to us he asks, "Have the police not been back to you?"

"No" was our reply... Tony says, "Come on Dunc, we have waited long enough for them to get here, we will go and get him out ourselves" and off they go, walking towards where we know Darrell is.

They have only been gone a few minutes when two police officers pull up beside our car. One asks me what is going on. I tell him Tony and Duncan have gone to get him, we were fed up of waiting.

"Wait here," he says, "We will go down to them." They drive off, blue lights flashing. I cannot see what is happening. It seems like forever when a text comes through from Duncan... 'COME AND SEE YOUR SON'.

I drive down the short distance like a woman possessed and pull up behind the police vehicle. Grab my phone, jump out and THERE HE IS!

Oh My God, what have they done to him? He looked like my dad, so much older than his 43 years. Filthy dirty, ripped clothes, fingerless gloves, cap and trainers, everything covered in horse manure. His face looked leathery, hair unkempt, teeth were a disgrace.

I said to him, "Darrell, how can you be like this? You are coming home with us. Show me where you have been living." We walked through the gates and headed towards the far end of the yard. He goes to a caravan in the corner, there are cats running out of it. I walk inside. You wouldn't let a dog live in it. Words cannot describe this Hell Hole that my son has been made to live in. I use my phone to take photographs. I'm lost for words; anger is building up inside me. What person could do this to another human being???

Darrell tells me there is no running water, toilet and a small halogen heater was the only warmth in a caravan, where the door didn't even close. We go outside, it's all still a bit confusing BUT I remember seeing a male and a female stood in the yard talking to Tony. The male was wearing a wool overcoat. That sticks in my mind. I approach the female and ask her if she has any children and how would she like her child treated like this? I'm really angry now and I want answers but Duncan asks me to calm down as they could have loads of travellers turn up to cause trouble and he proceeded to frogmarch me out the gates.

Duncan has, while this was all happening, got in touch with a news reporter, who sent down a photographer to take pictures of our reunion. I remember just hugging Darrell and feeling at peace at last. An officer approaches me as Darrell goes back into the farm. He says how sorry he is for the way Darrell has been treated. The next thing I remember is Darrell walking out with a black dustbin bag with clothes in and a pair of boots that looked way too big for him.

The police tell us to take Darrell home, so off we go! Duncan is driving, Darrell sat in the front, Tony and me in the back seat. The stench of Darrell's clothes is unbearable BUT we cope. We ask him so many things. Duncan says "Was that your holiday pay the big guy gave you? Darrell says,

"No, that's the first money I've had." "Well that was for the police, to make it look like they have paid you," I say.

I text close family and friends that we have got Darrell... Mobile is HOT with messages of Congratulations. I post on Missing Darrell Simester and Kidderminster Friends...

Ok, we will share our good news, WE HAVE OUR SON DARRELL BACK HOME... So this has been THE GREATEST DAY OF OUR LIVES! Please respect our privacy for the next few days; we have to let him recover. Many thanks for all your good wishes over the years and not giving up x x x you are wonderful people and I feel that I know you all. From the bottom of my heart, a VERY BIG THANK YOU... X X X

We get wonderful comments from hundreds of caring people.

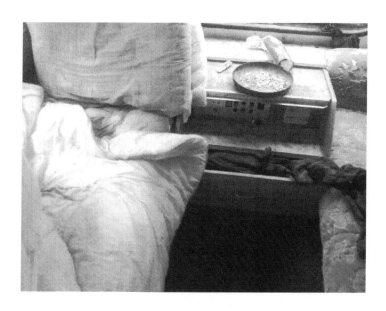

Jean Simester

The Hell Hole that my son was made to live in.

His 'Clothes'

Chapter 7

Darrell is in a Horrendous Condition Help!

On arriving home, we ask Darrell to have a shower. All his clothes he had on, go in a black bag. The trainers he was wearing and the boots he brought with him are left on the doorstep. Duncan goes off home, to get some clothes for Darrell. After Darrell comes out of the shower, Tony checks him over.

Tony shouts me and asks me to phone the doctors for an appointment - Darrell has a huge lump in his groin. After being away for thirteen years, there were many ailments. Darrell told us that he broke his hip, he fell from a horse. These scum, put him in a wheelbarrow and put him in his shed... two days before they took him to hospital, where they made him give a false name...

Tony took Darrell to our doctors. On arriving back Tony says, "That doctor was useless, can you make another appointment for tomorrow, with another doctor?" Which I did...

We need help but who will give us the help we need... I telephone social services, anyone I could find online... I'm trying to find someone...We are lost... What do we do?

On the Friday, Tony and I took Darrell to the doctor's. He treated us like we were invisible. He 'thinks' it could be a hernia but he's 'not sure'. A referral is made for an appointment for a scan.

The Welsh Echo writes a follow-up story about Darrell being found. The media are now phoning and knocking on our door... they all want our story now! On the Saturday morning, Darrell is in a lot of pain, with one thing and another. I phone the hospital and Tony takes Darrell for an 8.45am appointment. They tell him to go back if the pain gets worse...

The police arrive to see us. They want to take statements. Darrell is going to be taken to a 'safe house' but neither Tony, Duncan or I am allowed to go with him. It's got to be someone neutral, so Zoe says she will go with him. They go off, arriving back much later... Zoe comes in and bursts into tears. She is shocked at what she has heard, what Darrell had been through and how they had treated him.

The male officer in charge that day pulls me to one side and tells me he thinks Darrell is lying! WHOOPS! Wrong person to upset! Duncan did his statement at home. He hears something that is later 'denied' by police. Tony's statement is to be done at a later date, as he just cannot get his head around it all. Mine is arranged for me to go to Kidderminster Police Station the next day, (Sunday), in the afternoon. Later in the day, my mind goes over what the officer had said about Darrell. My mind's made up. I am NOT going to the station to do my statement, stuff them. If they want my statement, they can come to me.

On Sunday, rage is now taking over; I phone the hospital helpline. I explain about Darrell, where we have just rescued him from and I demand that 'someone' give him a 'Full Examination'. We get an appointment for 7.30p.m.

Sunday, late afternoon, I get a telephone call from the station, why had I not turned up?   I tell them, "I'm not coming, you can send someone here. Also, you can tell the officer who told me Darrell was 'lying', to stay away from me and my family. A lady officer arrives that evening and I give my statement.

Duncan arrives to take Darrell and I to the evening appointment, as Tony was not feeling well. We wait for nearly an hour to be seen. FOUR DAYS after we find Darrell, we actually get him checked over by a doctor. The report from this examination read: fever chills and rigors. Swelling right groin, poor feet, sore throat and back pain Hx of fall from a horse and was taken to hospital 2 days later for Rx hip which was pinned. Chronically ill-looking. Marked kyphosis of the thoracic. There is what appears to be an epidermoid cyst on the back. Mouth - poor oral hygiene with several carious teeth both top and lower rows. Gingival hyperplasia Pale + Anicteric. Chest – reduced air entry but no definite crackles. Abdomen – giant right Hernia with?? Hydrocele... Partially reducible. Right hip severe restriction in internal rotation, sec + ORIF Right hip. Left side SLR 80deg some mild restriction in ext. rotation 15 deg it side... Feet – severe Onychogryphosis Tinea Unguim. Soles of feet callosity – esp overhead of 1st MT. Throat – red – no exudates on tonsils. Left leg – erythema ab igne from close proximity to a hot surface.

DIAGNOSIS: Suspected Chest Infection. Poor dental hygiene – carious teeth. Malnutrition – suspected Osteoporosis. Secondary OA RT hip. Tinea Unguim. Callosity feet – needs podiatrist... Commence prophylactic antibiotic. See GP for continuing investigations for both Physical and Psychological Trauma.

EXAMINATION: Assessment.
DETAILS:
Oxygen Saturation 97.0%
Systolic Saturation BP mm Hg 110

Temperature 39.6
Diastolic BP mm Hg 59
Pulse bpm 77.

IT'S ONLY TAKEN 4 DAYS!!!
He has blood tests done and eventually a scan.

The 'police' start arriving in their droves. Funny how the West Midlands Police are keen to get in on the 'Action'! Crawling out of the woodwork. Our home is not our own. Darrell has to have photographs taken of his body. We don't know where to turn. I was expecting offers of help straightaway but I have to fight to get any. People just 'DO NOT' seems to believe you, that your son has been held as a 'SLAVE', they give you the opinion that you are 'OFF your rocker'.

Darrell has the scan on his groin. It is a HERNIA, equivalent to a size 3 football. We now have to wait to see the surgeon who will perform the operation. I have to take Darrell to an emergency dentist, again I have to explain. A couple of teeth are extracted. I get him registered at a local dentist, for other treatment.

Tony and I take him on a weekend break to the Lake District, to get a breather. Darrell suffers pain again in his teeth and he's very conscience of his bulge in his trousers from the hernia and always sits away from strangers. It's such a shame... I get the doctor to make a referral for the podiatrist, they don't really want to but I say I want his feet seen to. We have support visits, some are very helpful, some, as per normal, give you all the chat and that's all.

Chapter 8

The Police Finally Get Involved

Who can you trust?

The end of March 2013, Gwent Police get involved, Duncan and myself are still not 100% sure about trusting the police. After all, all we have ever had is lie, after lie, after lie, so who can blame us?

No arrests as yet, why? They, have to make a case...

A few weeks after we get Darrell home we give our story to a tabloid, to hopefully make people aware of slavery in this country... the photographer gets in touch a week after they had been to see us, he wants the postcode of the farm where Darrell had been... they are taking a helicopter over the farm to get aerial shots...

We are in total shock when we are shown the photos, for there in one of them is a man with a wheelbarrow working... Darrell says it is a man he called Cedric, a Polish guy, who sometimes worked there... Darrell had been told that he had gone back to Poland.

We show these photos and ask, "WHY has he not been rescued?" They say they are watching the farm, building the case... I am devastated...he's someone's son, husband, brother and they leave him there... I really cannot get my head around their thinking. Poor, poor man...

I'm asked to have all the photos I had taken put on a disc for evidence. I go and have this done in a computer shop. We are then told they cannot accept this and the mobile is the source and that's where they have to take them from. I am led to believe that I can stay with my phone as I have personal stuff on it... Duncan and I have to go to Hindlip headquarters in Worcester, we are met by 2 Gwent officers. One asks for all the items of clothing we have, that Darrell returned home with, these have to be individually put into a sealed bag. The other officer asked for my phone, he has to take it to one of their departments for the photos to be taken off. I explain, "I want to stay with my phone, it's got lots of info on that you should not see". I'm told that it won't take long... Well it took a few hours before I had my phone returned to me, they had taken everything off my phone... I am livid and I tell them both that they have invaded my privacy and I am not a happy bunny... I will not let it drop..

That same day, those two officers and the Superintendent in charge came to our home later. I tell them I have no respect for the police because of more lies... he apologises but the damage is done... We have questions we would like answered, do they answer truthfully? I don't think so... They tell us what they want, not what we want to hear.

Duncan has to take Darrell down to London, to see Dr Mike Korzinski. They go by train, just the one night... Dr Mike has been good for Darrell, he enjoys chatting with him. He has sessions both the Saturday and the Sunday before they return back home.

We are in May 2013; we still have no appointment for Darrell to see the surgeon for the hernia operation... I telephone our surgery and ask to speak with the doctor who referred him. He is on his day off, so I am put in touch with one of the other doctors. I tell her I am not happy and unless she gets Darrell an appointment that day, I was going to sit in her waiting room, until he gets one... She tells me she would get the secretary to phone the surgeon and find out when Darrell would be going to hospital.

I get a call back within half hour, to say he would be seen within a few days. When we see the surgeon we explain we would like Darrell to have a couple of days in hospital after the operation. He says yes, he can be in for 2/3 days because of the length of time the operation would take and it would help his recovery.

June 28th 2013. Hernia operation day. We have to travel roughly 18 miles to the hospital; we arrive at the specified time. We then wait six hours, before he's taken to the theatre. Operation takes two hours. We wait for him to come out. The surgeon tells us that all is ok BUT he had only ever seen a hernia that big on OLD men. Darrell had to have a 10 cm incision... We left him to rest; it's now 9pm on Friday night.

Next morning Darrell telephones to say he can come home... shock horror, it wasn't 24 hours and we had been told he would be in 2/3 days. We go and collect him. No discharge papers or any instructions as to what to look for, no pain relief, or dressing. We are now expected to be doctor and nurse.

Sunday 1st July 2013. Oh, what have we let ourselves in for? Our story is printed in The SUN on Sunday. The phone doesn't stop ringing, reporters knocking on the door, emails... Why, oh why, can't they leave us alone? Go chase those in Peterstone, they are the ones who need to be hounded and in the papers, for what they have done to Darrell. The police have had Tony's phone off him for nearly two months, to yet again, 'Take from the source'. They bring him another phone to use which looks like a child's play phone. I have now said that if anyone wants to visit us, it has to be on a Monday as I am sick and fed up with these do-gooders expecting to come 'whenever'.

All Clear, Lets Party. August 5th 2013, Darrell gets the all clear for his hernia operation.

So with lots of help from family and good friends, a party is organised...we have a room donated and gifts galore to raffle off. A big Welcome Home Party is all arranged for Saturday 10th August. 200 people come to wish him well, from Manchester, Wales and Blackpool... we have a fantastic night, with Darrell walking in with his brothers and sister to The Greatest Day... Many tears of happiness are shed, new friendships are made, people who had helped us immensely. Thank you to all those who came, you know who you are. We raised over £600 which we gave to Missing Adults and Children in the UK. As without their help, I honestly believe we would never have found him and he would have died in the most horrid conditions on that farm, shovelling horse s**t until he dropped dead, from being overworked, underfed and the freezing weather etc etc.

Chapter 9

The Gwent Police are still dropping in on us, STILL no arrests!!!

Social Services give Darrell a Care Worker. He's fantastic with Darrell, he takes him out and about, sometimes shopping and I am still fighting to get help. It's a welcome break for us, as we just do not have any time on our own. End of September, Darrell's Auntie Christine and Uncle Phil arrange for a night 'dog racing' in Manchester, a race is sponsored by them called "The Welcome Home Darrell Simester" race. He's over the moon... What a fantastic night. It was overshadowed by the press pinching photos off his Missing Darrell Simester page. So I had to make his page a closed item, to stop it happening again.

24th September 2013 'We get a phone call on the morning; this is going out in the news:

....Headlines....
Slavery probe latest: Home Secretary 'determined to tackle modern-day slavery'

Searches continue as the senior investigating officer appeals for the author of an anonymous letter to contact police. Home Secretary Theresa May has reiterated her determination to "tackle the scourge of modern-day slavery" as police investigation continues into a farm in South Wales.

A Home Office spokesman said "This is a shocking case and an appalling reminder of the extent to which slavery has reappeared in our country. The Home Secretary has made clear her determination to tackle the scourge of modern slavery and organised criminal gangs behind it. We are already taking action on a number of fronts. We are working with front-line professionals to help them better identify and support potential victims. The new National Crime Agency will, from next month, lead an enhanced and co-ordinated response to targeting trafficking gangs and we will be overhauling and updating legislation by bringing forward a draft Modern Day Slavery Bill this session."

Her statement came as an officer investigating alleged slavery and servitude at a farm at Peterstone, near Marshfield, today appealed for the writer of an anonymous letter to come forward. The senior investigating officer in the case made a personal appeal to the author of an anonymous letter which was sent to a neighbouring force some months ago to get in contact. The Detective Superintendent in charge said "The letter contains information which may be vital to this investigation and we need that person to contact us using the dedicated investigation number 01633 647174."

Officers today resumed their search at the Peterstone Farm as part of an ongoing inquiry into alleged slavery and servitude offences. Specialist officers, equipment and a forensic archaeologist have resumed the search for the body of an "unknown person" which may have been buried at the site. Gwent Police yesterday executed three early-morning warrants at a residential flat in Cardiff, a residential house in Penhow, Monmouthshire and at the Cariad Farm, Peterstone, near Marshfield, in an operation involving more than 100 officers.

Four people were later arrested, a 66 year old man and a 42 year old man, both from the Marshfield area; a 36 year old man from the Cardiff area; and a 42 year old woman from Penhow on suspicion of slavery and servitude offences. They remain in custody today, assisting officers with their inquiries following the granting of a superintendent's extension. The D.S in charge said "As a result of the publicity generated by the police activity I'm grateful to the people who have contacted us with information which is assisting our inquiry. Importantly we've received a number of calls from individuals who may also be potential victims or important witnesses. I'm urging those individuals to contact the investigating team again by ringing our dedicated number as we believe they may have more information which could be of assistance. Any information can be provided in complete confidence and officers and staff can provide any appropriate support. I would also urge anyone else who may have any other information relating to this investigation, no matter how unimportant it may seem, to pick up the phone and contact us.

"Alternatively if anyone has information and would rather not pass this directly to the police then I would urge them to contact Crime Stoppers, which is independent of the police and guarantees complete anonymity, on 0800 555 111. They don't need to give their name and the police will never know who they are. Any information given would be passed to the team in complete confidence."

Police had revealed a man of Eastern European origin, whose age was unknown, had been recovered from the Peterstone site and taken to an undisclosed medical reception centre. It is believed that he is a Polish national and he is currently being supported by specialist officers and the British Red Cross personnel.

A digger yesterday explored a manure heap as officers conducted ground searches in an adjacent field. They said the action came after an investigation prompted by the discovery of a man in Marshfield, who had been missing for 13 years, following a family appeal in March this year.

The RSPCA as well as a veterinary surgeon are also at the scene today to help ensure horses' wellbeing. The D.S. who is leading the investigation known as 'Operation Imperial', said the action was "the latest phase of a long-running investigation into offences of Slavery and Servitude".

He said "The investigation began when a 43 year old man was found to be living there, who had been reported missing by his family for 13 years. Since then a specialist team of detectives has been investigating and gathering intelligence to ascertain whether this is part of a larger criminal conspiracy. In addition to the suspected offence in relation to Slavery and Servitude, we are also acting on intelligence which suggests that a body of an unknown person may be buried at the Marshfield site. As such specially trained officers, equipment and a forensic archaeologist have been deployed to investigate this."

Neighbours in Peterstone have spoken of their shock at the police probe, which saw police set up a cordon outside the entrance to the farm and a number of specialist teams including a Scientific Investigation Unit descend on the site en masse.

One neighbour, who wanted to remain anonymous, said: "There was loads of police first thing this morning." Of those living at the property next door, she added "They have been there for years."

Another neighbour, who wanted to remain anonymous, said the heavy police presence and nature of the action was "very scary".

The D.S. added "Because of the scale of the investigation we are sorry the operation has caused disruption to other residents, especially in the Marshfield area and we thank them for their continued co-operation and understanding. Local officers are in the area to provide reassurance and if anyone has any concerns I would urge them to speak to these officers."

Gwent Police said a dedicated team of detectives had been responsible for the investigation which had centred on evidence and intelligence people were being kept in poor conditions at Marshfield and being forced to work for no pay. The force said they had been working in partnership with other forces, The Serious Organised Crime Agency (SOCA), UK Human Trafficking Centre, RSPCA and the Red Cross.

Members of the dog section, air support unit and armed response unit were among those to enter premises in relation to offences regarding Slavery and Servitude from the Criminal Law Act 1977 and the Coroners and Justice Act 2009. Gwent Police said today's operation began as a result of missing man Darrell Simester being found following an appeal.

After 13 years missing, Darrell, 43, was found in a tiny, mud-plastered two-berth caravan in Marshfield in March. His parents Jean and Tony, who live near Kidderminster in Worcestershire, had made a desperate plea for his return after learning he might be living in Cardiff. Described as "timid" and "vulnerable", Darrell was 30 when he went missing after running off into the night following an argument with friends while on holiday in Porthcawl. He was found by police a few days later sleeping rough under a hedge, but told them he was okay. A few days later, Jean and Tony had a call from two men who said Darrell was "working on the roads" with them.

In eight heart-rending years that followed, they heard from Darrell infrequently- as little as twice a year- and four years ago, on Christmas Eve 2008, the calls stopped for good. Jean, Tony and Darrell's siblings Brendan, 42, Duncan, 39, and

Zoe, 37, set up a Facebook group and contacted missing persons' charities but were told police couldn't help them because Darrell had been in touch and could therefore not be classed as a missing person.

Working with the help of a handful of Facebook followers, they finally traced the mobile number he first used to contact them, to a Cardiff firm and at the beginning of March an anonymous tip-off led them to a stable yard in Marshfield. They found Darrell living in a tiny mud-plastered caravan in a corner of a yard. A week later, police confirmed they were investigating the conditions in which he was "living and working" during his 13 years away from home.

Chapter 10

A Much Needed Holiday

November 2013. Darrell's siblings put together to send us to Tunisia, to celebrate Duncan's 40th. Vulnerable Adults helped us to get a passport for him; he's never flown before. We enjoy a lovely holiday away from it all.

December 2013. Christmas is drawing near, Darrell's first one at home since 1999 BUT it was spoilt by the news from Gwent Police that the two accused were out for Christmas, the news was like a death in the family, it was that bad.

Headlines South Wales Echo... Tuesday 14th January, 2014
' Man in court over Newport 'Slavery' case...

A man appeared before a judge yesterday charged with holding another man captive near Newport and enslaving him for more than a decade. The 37 year old man is accused of holding Darrell Simester against his will and forcing him into

Slavery between 2000 and 2013. He appeared on bail before
The Judge at Cardiff Crown Court.

He lived on Shirenewton caravan site, Wentloog Road,
faces a charge of kidnapping Mr Simester between August,
2000 and September 1st, 2000. He is also charged with
conspiring to hold Mr Simester in Slavery on February 1st,
2013. The defendant is also accused of false imprisonment
against Mr Simester by assaulting and injuriously
imprisonment between August 11, 2000 and March 1, 2013.
He was granted bail at an earlier hearing on November 21,
2013.

Yesterday, the Judge bailed him to a date to be fixed with
conditions including he does not contact prosecution
witnesses and stays at his home address.

Headlines South Wales Echo. Tuesday 21st January, 2014.
Slavery Probe...Gwent man cleared...

A Gwent man was cleared of requiring another to perform
forced or compulsory labour as the charge against him was
dropped. He pleaded not guilty to the charge at Cardiff Crown
Court this morning. He spoke only to confirm his name and
deny the charge. Prosecution offered no evidence against the
accused, so the Judge dismissed the case against him.

Headlines South Wales Echo. 30th January, 2014.
Slavery Probe: Father and son to stand trial

A father and son will stand trial after they denied requiring another man to perform forced or compulsory labour at a farm near Newport. Both men from Cariad Farm, Peterstone, Near Newport, both denied the allegation, said to have taken place against Darrell Simester between April 6th, 2010 and March 1st, 2013, at a hearing at Cardiff Crown Court today. Trail was scheduled for March 17th, 2014. Both men were released on bail.

Headlines South Wales Argus. Monday 17th February 2014
'Newport father and son will face slavery trail in autumn'

Today a father and son were told at Cardiff Crown Court that they will face trail over alleged Slavery in the autumn. A Judge has put back the opening of a trail of two men alleged to have enslaved a man to the autumn. They are charged with holding a man captive and enslaving him over more than a decade. The trail was due to open on March 17th but today the Cardiff Judge set a new trial date for September 15th.

The Family from Cariad Farm, off Wentloog Avenue, Peterstone, appeared on bail at Cardiff Crown Court today (February 17). The trail is expected to last 25 court days, the Judge said. The elder person is charged with one count of false imprisonment against Darrell Simester in Newport between August 2000 and March 1st, 2013. He is charged with conspiring to hold Mr Simester in slavery in Newport between April 6th, 2010 and March 1st, 2013. He is also charged with conspiring to require Mr Simester to do forced labour in Newport. The younger person is charged with false imprisonment against Mr Simester in Newport between August 10th, 2000 and March 1st, 2013. He is charged with conspiring to hold Mr Simester in slavery in Newport between April 6th 2010 and March 1st, 2013. He is also charged with conspiring to require Mr Simester to perform forced labour in Newport between April 6th, 2010 and March 1st, 2013.

The Judge granted the two bail.

Chapter 11

We are Falling Apart...

Twelve Months On. Tony and I have been married nearly 45 years and we are finding life to be so hard. The pressure we are going through is tearing us to pieces. Tony is having regular sessions with Victim Support. Darrell is in his own little world, if he is doing what he likes, he's happy. If not he is like a stroppy teenager. This annoys Tony. Me, well I'm still trying to keep the peace and I'm Piggy in the Middle, cannot do right for doing wrong.

We have asked our doctor for a 'Learning Assessment'. A referral was sent off; the reply was to be told that he 'doesn't fit the criteria' even though he has never met him. We ask for a 'Needs Assessment', a young woman comes twice, asking questions about this, that and the other, only for her to tell us he 'doesn't fit the criteria'? Parts of the assessment were not to my liking, bad grammar, poor spellings and at times not even correct, so I complain and say I want another assessment done.

More and more people are coming to visit, we had 3 young women come from Sandwell Women's Aid, and (via the Salvation Army) apparently they should have come with support as soon as we brought Darrell home. They arrive April/May 2014. They can only give you six weeks, we saw them 3 or 4 times, that was all.

So many faces and names...

They all come with good intentions, giving advice, (some - and they know who they are - are brilliant at their job). But hey, they haven't had to live our lives since August 2000. They think they know all the answers but haven't got a clue what's gone on over 13 years, while Darrell has been missing, or the hassle, stress, the sorting things out yourself, over the last sixteen months BECAUSE No One Really Cares. As long as we do it, it's 'carry on, you are doing a good job'.

Darrell goes to a drop-in centre every Tuesday, we take him and drop him off and collect him for the first few weeks until he feels ok. He starts to use the bus service and goes to a betting shop, nearly every day, he doesn't gamble big, just pence but he still goes near enough every day. This starts to aggravate Tony and Duncan, until tempers are now raw. Here I am again, in the middle. Trying to keep the peace.

Arguments are a regular thing and with emotions high, Tony's had enough, he leaves home and stays the night at Zoe's, on the sofa, then books himself into a B&B. Things are tough, we have been married 45 years and this happens, but it won't be the last time. A few weeks later Tony leaves again, he stays at Duncan's for one night and says he won't be back until Darrell has gone.

Duncan telephones Gwent Police, who contacts Wyre Forest Community Housing who say he can have two nights in a B&B. At The Collingdale in Kidderminster, Duncan takes Darrell and drops him off.

This place is a right doss hole... Darrell doesn't deserve to be there. We are advised to take Darrell to the Hub on the Monday morning and register him as homeless, which we do, only to be told to take him to the housing association later that morning. We arrive ten minutes before our appointment, only to be kept waiting forty minutes. Things don't go well, it angers me and I'm fed up with people not knowing what's gone on and how Darrell has been treated.

We ask the housing association for help, to find Darrell a place of his own. He is on their waiting list but that's no good for us. We need help with a home for him straightaway. (It seems that as Darrell had been 'Trafficked' they should have provided him with a property.) They offer him a B&B, it's full with people who took drugs or were drop-outs, not the place for a Vulnerable Person. NO ONE GIVES A SHIT!!

What he has been through, I thought they would be jumping through hoops to help..

We are told there was nowhere else for Darrell to go, only the Collingdale. We say he is not going back there and bring Darrell back home, much to the annoyance of Duncan, and he tells us he wants no contact with us until Darrell has his own place, as it is all down to Darrell that we are arguing.

Darrell was put back into the Collingdale on Friday 6th June to 10th June. This time I took photographs of this disgusting place. Hypodermic needles in the room... I report it to the housing, trading standards and the British Tourism. It needs closing down. Just because someone is homeless, it doesn't constitute sending them to a place like this.

Darrell is now in another B&B in Stourport on Severn, he has been there since 10th June, 2014. He will stay there until his bungalow is available. Hopefully only a few weeks.

Tony is beside himself, he threatens not to eat, drink or take his medication. What am I to do? No one gives a toss about how we are coping. Life is shit to put it mildly. I am now sick and fed up with the do-gooders, they do not understand what our lives have been and are like. I'm at my wits' end, I wish I was dead; I take 16 x 500mg Paracetamol over a few hours, just want to deaden the pain I am in.

Learning Assessment is a 'No Go, NO FUNDS' (if this government did not keep giving foreigners, there would be funds for English Citizens) even though we have our suspicions that Darrell is autistic, we just want it confirmed and to get professional help, how to understand, how to help Darrell and cope with it.

We get the second Needs Assessment done by a more mature lady, who has met Darrell a few times. The assessment form with her findings are posted to us, she and her line manager come to see us with the news that Darrell doesn't need help! BUT then after reading two paragraphs in the Analysis & Outcomes she has written. He is still vulnerable and easily influenced by others and might be taken advantage of. He is willing and eager to please others. He has previously been taken advantage of by a friend at the drop-in centre. Also, Darrell requires support to deal with situations that he cannot manage on his own, such as saying 'NO' to people. He is still unable to protect himself from others and is anxious about going to town on his own.

So WE ARE going to get some help with Darrell?

I am driving Darrell to Barbourne Medical Centre in Worcester each Wednesday afternoon for counselling. 12 sessions paid for by Victim Support, which I asked for, and it was sorted within 24 hours. We couldn't get any sessions from the NHS.

I hate people telling me 'Do this' and 'Do that'! Well YOU 'do this, do that'. We are just parents who want the best for Darrell, WHY should we have to 'do this, do that'? YOU are supposed to be 'THE PROFESSIONALS'. DO NOT tell us what to do, if you are not prepared to do the same. YOU get PAID to do your job, not us.

Anything we have asked for usually gets a NO, so we have to do it ourselves, we are 63 & 67 and should be enjoying our retirement, relaxing and being happy BUT this is not happening; our marriage is on the rocks, if we can get back to normal, who knows? The last 16 months should have been happy but we have only had heartache, pain and agony because of the lack of support from Social Services, Doctors Housing etc. So for all those who have come and gone and I suspect many more will come and go.

We have the court case to look forward to in September, this should have been over and done with but the Judge wanted his jollies and put it back 6 months. Let's hope we get the RESULT we would like.

In May 2014, I have to take Darrell to WORCESTER Hospital for a bone density scan, to be told by our doctor, a couple of weeks later that Darrell has osteoporosis of the spine, he now has to take medication for this, as well as a vitamin tablet daily. What Darrell has been through, we don't know, as he does not share his thoughts. So why do people not give a shit, he surely is owed something good to happen. What sort of society are we?

Darrell finally gets his own bungalow, in August 2014. He is so proud, some new items, some donated by family and friends, all wanting to help him get on with his life. On September 1st 2014 we travelled to Cardiff, for a pre trial tour of the Crown Court

On September 1st, 2014, we travelled down to Cardiff for a pre-trial tour of the Crown Court and we go and meet some of the Operation Imperial team at their headquarters and are shown around and see the work they are doing.

Are we in for a shock!!!!

The superintendent in charge tells us he has a confession... the police had in 2011 been to the farm where Darrell was held, over an incident and asked who he was, and because they said he was family, they never interviewed Darrell. We are gobsmacked to say the least... I'm in tears. I cannot believe what we have just been told. (What chance have we got of getting THEM sent to prison?)

Court is getting nearer... The BBC want to do a documentary on Darrell and Slavery. So we arrange to travel to Wales, to start being interviewed and recorded. All very scary but we have to get our story out in the media.

Trial beings, the end of September. The CPS put us up in a hotel in Cardiff, for Darrell's evidence over Tuesday, Wednesday, Thursday and Friday. He is totally drained, so are we! On the following Monday, Darrell has to finish his evidence, then Duncan and myself give ours. 'They' are sat a few feet away. I hate them so much, I want to see them sent to prison, the longer the better. There is no court for the rest of the week until Friday, when we drive down for Tony to give his evidence. The following week, we get a call from our barrister, the son will plead guilty, as he says his dad wasn't there all the time and did not know what was going on, on the farm. I am gutted, I wanted it to go to the jury, I want those responsible put inside.

After all the stress, I am ill in bed, doctor has to come to visit me. I'm given antibiotics and steroid medication... can't eat... I feel really awful. We are notified by the police that sentencing is 24th October, 2014 at Cardiff Crown Court. Close family and friends want to support us on the day, two of my girlie friends from Missing Adults and Children in UK join us at court. One travelling from Lancashire, to be with us. I still am feeling under the weather but I have to be there to see this 'B*****d sent down. Tony pleads with me not to go.

4.5 years is clearly not enough for what 'he'/'them', put Darrell through. Will probably be out in two years... Where is the justice?

Straight after court we have to go to put the finishing touches to the documentary, with the BBC... then we have to travel back home... feeling drained. I cannot believe the sentence, some law from 6th April, 2010 was all that he could be charged for.

Chapter 12

I have researched this about Slavery...

...SLAVERY was banned in 1833 all over Britain...

William Wilberforce was an English Politician who became the voice of the abolition movement in Parliament. He met James Ramsey in 1784 and for the first time, discussed Slavery. He championed many causes but it was the fight against The Slave Trade that he worked most tirelessly for. From 1789, Wilberforce regularly introduced bills in Parliament to Ban the Slave Trade. He was fiercely opposed by those making fortunes from the Trade, who used all kinds of delaying tactics. The first time a bill was introduced, Wilberforce lost the debate by 163 votes to 88 but he NEVER GAVE UP. A bill to cease the trade was passed by The House of Commons in 1792 - but with the amendment that the ban should be gradual, which those with an interest in the Trade interpreted as 'never'.

Finally on 25th March, 1807, the Abolition of The Slave Trade Act abolished the Slave Trade in the British Colonies. It was carried by 267 votes. The house rose to its feet and cheered wildly. William Wilberforce continued to work for the abolition of all Slavery within the British Colonies. On the 26th July, 1833, the abolition of Slavery bill was passed, its third reading in the House of Commons. Just three days later on 29th July, William Wilberforce died.

Note:-

Slavery was completely abolished in 1833 (in the British Empire). Yet it apparently wasn't necessary to abolish it in homes. Until the 6th APRIL, 2010, however, which is when all Slavery was banned in the UK, with jail of up to 14 years in prison.

Headlines 26th October. Wales Online

'Man held as a slave for 13 years thought he would never see his family again'

Darrell Simester was tricked into believing that his parents were dead but the reality was they had never given up looking for him. The man who was kept as a slave on a South Wales Farm has spoken about his 13 years of torment and how he was made to work from 6.30am to 5pm without a break. Timid Darrell Simester had to sleep in a rat-infested shed and wash in a horse trough after working 15 hour days for no pay on Cariad Farm outside Newport.

The man who forced him to work for well over a decade - while his family had no idea what had happened to him - was jailed last week for 4.5 years. He weighed just 8 stone and had a bent spine, chest wall deformity, tooth decay and a hernia the size of a football.

The 45 year old told the Sun on Sunday "People think slavery ended hundreds of years ago but I'm proof it's happening in the 21st century. I thought I'd never be free but my family never gave up looking." In fact it was a desperate plea last year by his parents Tony and Jean, in the South Wales Echo that led to him being found. It said they feared their 'timid' and 'easily led' son was being held in the area against his will. A week later someone tipped off the police and Mr Simester was found on the farm.

* This last paragraph is not correct, mistake by the writer of this story*

His ordeal began in August 2000, when he chose to hitchhike 120 miles home after a row during a caravan holiday in Porthcawl. The person in question and another man pulled over and offered him some work but Darrell said "I replied 'no thanks, I want to get home' but they dragged me on the truck. I wish I'd put up more of a fight but they weren't people you want to mess with." When they got back to the farm, near Newport Darrell said "He showed me the shed where I'd sleep. After an hour he came back with a shovel and wheelbarrow and told me to get to work." It was some of what was to follow for the next 13 years, with up to 15 hours a day working.

He said "At 6.30am, I started mucking out 150 horses, with no break until 5pm. At 5.30pm, someone would bring stew before I locked up at 6pm and began watching over the farm. Early on I made a mistake with the horses. He threw a shovel at my head which missed by an inch, I was too scared to ask for wages, clothes or medicine."

Darrell was only allowed two phone calls a year from 2000 to 2008 but he (The Person charged) was always standing nearby telling Darrell what to say. Darrell was even tricked into believing that his parents were dead but his mum said that having him back was amazing. She said "That hug after 13 years was like winning the lottery".

Chapter 13

4th November 2014
BBC 1 Wales 'Week in Week out
Documentary
Headline reads..."Newport 'slavery' victim
Darrell Simester speaks of ordeal"

It was a case that lifted the lid on modern day 'slavery' in Wales. The accused was jailed last month for forcing a vulnerable man to work unpaid at a farm near Newport. Now as BBC Wales' Week in Week out programme delves further into the case, we take a look at some of the issues raised.

*Victim Darrell Simester and his family speak about his ordeal for the first time.

*Police reveal vulnerable people are being targeted by traveller gangs to work for free.

*An anthropologist looks at why some travellers have 'dependant servants'

*A BBC reporter who was at the scene when Mr Simester was found recalls what   happened.

Week in Week out Darrell's Story - BBC Wales 10.35pm 4th November 2014

(We sit and watch, tears streaming from us both. I'm ill yet again.) Think it might be the release of the past months.

A vulnerable man who was forced to work unpaid on a farm for 13 years has spoken for the first time about his ordeal. Darrell Simester, 44, had been made to work for up to 16 hours a day at Cariad Farm in Peterstone near Newport, only ever having two days off. He lived in appalling conditions, first in a rat-infested shed then a cold, squalid caravan, with only a horse trough to wash in and no soap or toothbrush.

The accused, 42, who is from a traveller family, was jailed for four-and-a-half years after pleading guilty to forcing Mr Simester to perform forced or compulsory labour.

Speaking of the moment the farmer was sentenced at Cardiff Crown Court, Mr Simester told BBC Wales' Week in Week out programme; I wished he'd have got 13 years for what I'd gone through. "Living in a shed, then a caravan, in those cold, damp nights, freezing cold and frightened as well. In my heart every day I was thinking, I wonder what happened to the rest of my family. Just kept going over in my head and in my stomach every day I was on that horrible horrible farm."

Mr Simester's family, from Kidderminster in Worcestershire, believed he was missing after going on a trip to the seaside in Porthcawl in South Wales in 2000. In fact, a member of the accused's family had picked him up at the side of a dual carriageway while travelling home and taken him to the family farm.

After his family finally tracked him down early last year following a social media campaign, they hardly recognised him, describing him as being a "broken man" who looked far older than his years. Mr Simester's father Tony, who had feared his son, was dead, told Week in Week out, "I went, that's not my son; that's not my son. But as he got closer and looked up, cause he walked towards me with his head bowed, I could see it was my son."

His mother Jean added, "I just said 'You're coming home. You can't stay here' and it was like winning the lottery; getting my arms around him and giving him a hug."

As the accused was jailed, the Judge told him, the way he had treated his victim was "repellent and wrong" and "not much better than a slave."

Mr Simester, who was left malnourished, with a chest infection, a hernia and calloused feet after his time at Cariad Farm, is continuing to rebuild his life and now has his own place to live. When asked what he wanted in the future, he replied, "A wife and a couple of kids."

Police investigating the Simester case say a pattern is emerging across the UK involving criminals from the travelling community exploiting vulnerable adults for their own benefit. The DS in charge of Gwent Police said "they were deliberately, often homeless men, at specific places and forcing them into labour. Whether they are shelters, park benches, or other locations where they would congregate but similarly those suspected of these offences would be able to target different people for their own means."

Michael Stewart, a social anthropologist who has worked and lived with traveller families, said "Most travellers treated their workers well but in Mr Simester's case it was clearly exploitative and abuse. What's certainly true is that travellers are not highly thought of," said Mr Stewart, who says he does not speak for travellers but has studied them and tried to see things from their point of view. Travellers are often despised, not many people would go and live in a traveller's compound on a traveller site. So to some extent you could say the labour market is restricted. So travellers tend to pick up people who are less able to find a position in the mainstream labour market.

"Sometimes those relationships, it's quite clear from the court cases there have been, have become exploitative and abusive. In other occasions, in other places and in other families, those relationships can be protective and supportive." He added, "It's certainly true that in some cases for traveller families having dependent servants who are non-travellers is a form of demonstrating wealth and status and achievement and you have the space to house these people, you have the social pulling power in a sense, that you're an attractive enough proposition."

David Phillips, Chief Executive of South Wales Race Equality Council, which speaks for traveller families: "We recognise that this is not what happened on this occasion and our communities are as horrified as everybody else at Mr Simester's treatment," said Mr Phillips.

Clare Hutchinson is a Researcher at Week in Week out and has followed Mr Simester's story since he was found. "I first spoke to Darrell Simester's mum Jean, in February 2013. I worked at a local newspaper and she sent us a long heartrending email explaining that she was looking for her son who had been missing for 13 years, she believed he was in South Wales. When I picked up the phone and spoke to her, I had little idea how far the story would go. Jean was heartbroken and desperate for someone to help her family in their hunt for Darrell - a search that had already gone on for more than a decade and involved dozens of meetings with police that always ended with officers telling her he was a 'missing contact' not a 'missing person'. In her words to me during that first phone call, 'He's not a missing contact, he's my son.' Jean and her husband Tony described their son, who would now be 43, as 'timid' and 'easily led'.

"They also told me of their suspicions that he was being held against his will somewhere in Cardiff. He had gone on holiday with another family in August 2000 and after an argument had run away. A few days later they heard from him: he was working on the roads. For eight years he would call a couple of times a year, often with voices in the background telling him what to say.

"Then in 2008, Darrell called his family at Christmas. He promised to speak to them again in the New Year - but that phone call never came. We ran a story in the newspaper in which Jean and Tony made a desperate plea for anyone who recognised Darrell to come forward. It was a last ditch attempt after 13 years of searching but – incredibly - it paid off. A few days later, Jean's mobile phone rang and the person at the other end told her they had seen Darrell working on a farm on the Gwent levels between Newport and Cardiff.

"I was in work on a rainy morning in late February 2013 when I got a tearful phone call from Jean saying they may have found Darrell - and that they were on their way down to Cardiff. I rushed out and met Jean, Tony and Darrell's younger brother, Duncan, outside Cariad Farm just as the police arrived. The family had not known what to expect - or even whether the man would be their son. Duncan approached him first but when Darrell told him he could not leave the farm the family were suspicious enough to call the police. Officers arrived a short while later - and wearing torn, filthy clothes, a flat cap and carrying his worldly goods in a black bin bag, Darrell emerged from the farm."

Darrell has his first Christmas in his new home, Christmas tree with chocolates and candy sticks, just like his Gran used to have. Shopping for presents, all wrapped up under the tree. Lights in his window. He is so proud and so are we, of what he has achieved in a short time. New Year's Day, Darrell puts on a buffet for the family. He's like a child in a sweet shop, all excited. He put on a buffet. Done us proud.

After lots of letter writing to the NHS, most times to the point of threatening to slap the next person who tells me 'he doesn't fit the criteria'. They have never met him and yet they think they have the right to judge him. Eventually the NHS

refers us to Worcestershire County Council for an
ASSESSMENT, at The Family Psychologist in Droitwich.
Four parts of assessment for Darrell to do and one for Tony
and myself.

Ours was all about Darrell growing up, how he was at
school, what friends he had. So hard when you have got four
children, all so very different. Forty plus years to go through.
But we do our very best...

Chapter 14

28th February 2015, Two Years at Home

Here are a few of the well-wishers' comments on 'Missing Darrell Simester', as I say we are going to write a book and if they would like to contribute.

Kat Foy: From Missing Adults and Children in the UK.

Met you by chance after my eyes were opened to how many Missing People we have in the UK. I became part of a 'Missing' page; I had only been on the page a couple of days. Early one morning a lady posted a message to her son, it blew me away reading it. I got to know an amazing lady, who had so much courage, guts and hope. I started following your journey. Darrell had been missing from home nearly 12 years, you had the most amazing strength and taught ME so much, you never once gave up on finding Your Son, you and Tony knew Darrell had JUST not gone Missing, you both knew there was something wrong. Then came the Story that led to Darrell, you were totally Right, he had been kept in the most appalling conditions, treated so badly. When I received the News you were with Darrell my heart was pounding, I was so happy for you, then came the awful state Darrell was in, he had been treated so bad and horrendous injuries but still showed the most amazing courage. I was asked to attend Darrell's Home Coming. I was so nervous when I arrived but you put me at ease, meeting you and Darrell and Tony was the most amazing experience I have had. Darrell is such a gentle man with an amazing smile and lived this horrendous experience that most couldn't live. Over the months leading up to The Trial you allowed me to stay on Your Journey. I know I could never deal with the heartache, pain and suffering you all went through. Being at The Sentencing I saw a True Hero. You all changed my life, opened my eyes and my heart, and taught me what goes on in life and how Slavery DOES EXIST. I am so very proud and humble, you allowed Me to be part of Your journey and gave Me what I have in my heart, you taught Me to believe and NEVER GIVE UP. I owe you all so very much...

Lizann Carran:

Hi Jean, I did post as I came across Darrell's Story and was overjoyed that he came back safe, to be with those he loved. It highlighted the plight of people in our Country, alone, afraid, enslaved, imprisoned and so much more. Starved of the basic Human Rights and things taken for granted - like the support of loved ones, a clean warm bed, food, clothing, shelter, dignity, safety and security. It made my year when Darrell got back home safely. I hope the many messages of love and support, that he and your family received, hopefully restored some of your faith in the World around us. I'm so glad you are all writing his Story..... It needs to be heard.

With much love to you all

Liz x x

Laura Bowater:

This is a lovely thing to do Jean, it will help raise awareness. I think the positive thing to come out of your book, is that you never gave up after all those years. You put all your dedication into finding your son and it paid off. Not only is he safe now but he's living a life, now, that he truly deserves, with the love and support of your family. The support network you had on here was fab; we were all behind you, hoping for the same result. You're a true inspiration to Darrell, your Husband, family and everyone else that is going through the same heartbreak you went through x x x The one message to come out of this, is NEVER GIVE UP !

Kerry Corns:

I'm disgusted that it still goes on and no-one had any idea, that your lad was held 'Captive' because that is the right word. I'm so glad he was found and these despicable people were / are dealt with. The healing process may take a while but with the right help and love off you and the rest of the family Darrell will recover. It makes you wonder how on earth in this alleged civilized country, how cruel some people are. They are 'Bullies' choosing their 'Victims' in order to destroy confidence and self-esteem, to mould them into 'Slaves'. I could go on and on about this but the most important thing is, Darrell was found and I really do hope he has some kind of normality. As a mother, we protect our children, no matter what age and the helplessness we feel when we can't is enormous but never giving up, gives us the strength to believe we can see light at the end of the tunnel. I wish you all well and anyone else who is in this predicament will know that giving up is NEVER an option. Good Luck with book that in itself will help heal.

Andrea Preece:

I was shocked Jean when I heard Darrell was missing. I knew him from school, he was in the same class at Harry Cheshire as my big brother Andrew. I knew Darrell as being a quiet, caring and genuine lad. To discover he was missing really did concern myself and when spreading the word, others who knew him. When finding out that he'd been found, it was such a relief but also hearing what Darrell had been through sickened myself and my family, as we knew Darrell, as being absolutely used and abused. Slavery in the Country was generally something people wanted to ignore, or believe it doesn't happen. You and your family had the strength and courage from Darrell, enabled people to become more aware and even though both Andrew and myself haven't seen Darrell since leaving school, he will be forever on our minds. Out of heartbreak, has come strength and courage and shows a loving family, determined to get through this. Love always x x x I'm glad you had the strength to support Darrell in Court Proceedings as well, it was needed to stop this happening again, you as a family are inspiring Jean x x x x

Pat Newey:

Jean, I cannot imagine what you and the family have been through. As a mom myself I can understand your pain and frustration but it really was a miracle the way that Darrell was found. You all are an inspiration to us all.

S.R.E:

Jean, I think it's hugely raised awareness and will continue to do so by writing a book, I found it personally 'Barbaric' and totally scary that this STILL goes on and so close to our 'normal' everyday lives. The fact you never gave up hope and faith within your own family and generally to get him back was incredible and shows your bravery and courage. You are amazing people and part of the healing process of you all will be to do this. You may also give others hope and courage, to have the same strength and faith as you. It's so cruel and horrific what he endured and by writing your story, you may help others but as I say, also bring awareness for us all, to be vigilant to these treacherous and vile ways that others inflict on the vulnerable. Bless you all and I am so glad you are all moving on. You are incredible... I myself and my family have been through enormous trauma in our lives and would too like to make people aware. It's the only way forward in order to heal. Enormous love to you all x x x x

....

April 2015

A little faith and a show of love from a lovely, elderly, Gentleman from Wales. He sends us a letter written from his heart, how he felt. He told us about his life and that he was writing a 'Poem' for Darrell and would be bringing it to Kidderminster Police's Vulnerable Adults. This is his Poem, which he framed:

A Tribute to Darrell Simester of Kidderminster,
Lost for 13 years! Found and returned to his home.

The fair county of Worcester t'was where it began
Our Darrell said, "Yes dad I am off to make a fresh start I am"
And hitching a ride he was soon in Porthcawl.
In South Wales, with friends, most surprised by the call
"twas not to be, just sun and sand
Where Darrell thought he would try his hand."
It did not last we learnt, so on the road again.
Hoping for a ride perhaps? To help ease the pain,
Darkness fall, the hedgerow beckons enough for I'll take a rest
Tomorrow is another day, I'll pace myself tis best
Bet now what luck, a stranger stops to ask
I'll give you shelter, work too if you are up to the task
And so it came to pass that poor Darrell's dream
Ended here at the roadside unaware of an evil scheme
Which, trapped the poor boy, into the life of a slave.
Twas lucky, poor Darrell avoided an early grave
His maker and mine with a firm guiding hand
Was there, unseen to care and protect that land
Where he toiled each day no questions asked
Just work, work work the endless task
And all the while, a search was instigated
By mum and dad, it was quite complicated
They fought on, with hope and put their trust in "Him"
Not knowing, but praying that in the end they would win
And so it was that this poor boy was found
Only just in time, almost "out" on the ground

The Lord works in mysterious ways, but now after many
days
He was spotted in the yard, with a barrow working hard
Recognised by his dad shouting, "Mother we've found our
lad!"
I think our search is done, we are about to rescue our son
And Darrell now is quite safe, back home, his rightful
place
His suffering and endless misery bravely borne
Now a bath, a shave, new clean clothes will be worn
We all hope Darrell can forget the past
And enjoy his future days, free at last!
From his cruel master's ways, now in jail counting his
days.
Never more to treat a human being so
For sure "it's to hell he will go"
Now Darrell "your adventure is over"
You forget the past now live in clover
And may God Bless you always.

....

Many thanks to this Gentleman for sharing his thoughts
with us, we really do appreciate it. There are some good
people in this world, not all are bad...x x

July 13th 2015 YES.... We get the result of the Autism
Assessment...Yes Darrell is autistic, with mild learning
difficulties and behaviour problems. I'm over the moon, tears
flow. We were right all along and The Professionals were
WRONG... The doctor from the clinic tries to explain it the
best way she can from the 27 page report. She explains who
WE need to contact, (whoops, been here before. Just get on
with it Jean, at least you know it will be sorted.)
Eventually I get the W.C.C. Social Services and get a Care
Plan sorted. Case to the IPCC is dragging their feet,
something else to chase up. Not happy as we have not been
kept up to date on this investigation. Life is good at the time

of putting pen to paper, something is bound to upset me though !!!

Something is still bugging me. Looking back through all the paperwork, I find letters from Theresa May MP, Baroness Randerson. Then on 31st July, 2015 the government announce that the New Slavery Law is now in use! The lady on TV is a Karen Bradley MP, so I'm on a mission, as I think that the Slavery of 1833 that was passed by government, should have been used. So I email her... I get three emails from her...

I myself do not think that this government really care what goes on with Slavery. They just live in their own little 'Safe' bubble. It will never happen to their families, they don't live in the 'Real' world. Until it does, their attitude to Slavery WILL NOT change.

Modern Day Slavery IS, very much, going on in this country and all over the WORLD. It could be happening near you! It's appalling, that it does. These people know who to choose as their Slave, they are abhorrent individuals, they do not deserve to be allowed to live and treat human beings the way they do.

They get caught; they either get off, as 3 of them did in Darrell's case or 4.5 years as Darrell's perpetrator did and now behind bars, being treated better than he EVER treated my son. He will more than likely be released in 2-2.5 years. I wish he would ROT in a filthy rat-infested hole, where he belongs, even that would be too good for him.

My Hate for HIM, his family and the likes of them is immense. I wish I was younger and I could really get me on a mission to show people what, these 'Horrible' low life, up, for what they are. They even lied about their names, to throw us off finding them. Who knows, someone may read our book and contact me?

My thoughts to those involved....

Friends on Facebook's 'Missing Darrell Simester': Without your support, love and encouragement, we may never of found him. Thank you all. x

Missing Adults and Children in the UK: Jan Sullivan, sadly passed away April 2014 and won't get to read our book. R.I.P. Many thanks for all you did with giving your time to post Alerts and Pics for me, the endless times I've had a moan and you have listened to me and gave me enormous support, which kept me going.

Clare Hutchinson: Many, many thanks to you, the Welsh Echo and BBC ONE Wales. We all appreciate what you have done.

Police: I still have little or no respect for them, we did their job for them, in searching and finding Darrell and photographic evidence I took, clothes I kept, that Darrell came home in on the day, goes to show how incompetent they are. We have only had contact with them 3-4 times since the sentencing. It's like we have been forgotten in my eyes. IPCC is ongoing, they have to be held responsible for their actions. We did not deserve to be treated the way we were.

Drs and Hospitals: need to be made more aware that Slavery is here and now and their attitudes need to change.

Social Services and Housing Associations: need to appreciate that any person who has been trafficked, needs help immediately, not treated as a second class citizen.

Kidderminster Vulnerable Adults and Victim Support: Thank you, you have been helpful in many ways and I am grateful for meeting you all.

The Court and Sentencing: What can I say here, OK, he, (Doran), got 4.5 years, which was a complete and utter insult to Darrell, the Slavery Law was passed in the 19th Century not 2010, you cannot have a Law passed in government and ignore it. He (Doran) should be doing at the least 13 years... 'An eye for an eye'. Or better still LIFE.

We have had to FIGHT, SHOUT and STAMP our feet to get anything done to help Darrell. No-one should have to do this, it should all be offered. It's just ignorance on the services out there. 'Ignorance is bliss.' I have stayed strong enough to cope, I will stay strong, as long as I have to. Writing this book, has brought back so many memories, some very bad ones, which has had me crying while trying to write BUT I have wonderful happy memories that outweigh the bad ones.

To those of you who I have met on this journey, I can only say, a VERY BIG THANK YOU. You have probably had me talk your ears off, with my relenting chatting about searching for Darrell. You have all given me the strength to persevere and carry on.

I am so sorry to my Beloved Tony, Brendan, Duncan, Zoe and their families for being obsessed with searching for Darrell but I would have done exactly the same, if it had been one of you. To Darrell, I hope you have a wonderful life and can hopefully put all that has happened to you to rest. I hope the pain and suffering eases with time. You all have my unconditional love, forever.

Wishing you all love, happiness and peace.

Jean x x x

Chapter 15

This chapter is written by Darrell's dad.

This story is about a man of 30 years of age, who went on holiday with some so-called friends and who never returned for 13 years.

In the book there are contributions from Darrell's parents, Darrell himself, Darrell's youngest brother, friends and even people who do not know the family but people who followed the story on Facebook or in the papers and who would now like to help with the slavery situation in the UK.

The police did not know how bad the situation was until we found Darrell 28th February, 2013. It is beyond belief that they will admit that they made mistakes when the day came that we tracked Darrell down, went to Wales to see if it really was him and actually found him on Cariad Farm, Peterstone, in South Wales.

In a newspaper they wrote:

Englishman who vanished 13 years ago discovered working as slave on farm.

Darrell Simester, now 43, was discovered starved, suffering a deformed spine, infected feet and missing teeth after allegedly working 365 days of the year from dawn to dusk. He disappeared while on holiday and said he was too afraid to run away from the men who had taken him in.

The Sun reports no sign of the farm's owners at the property on Sunday. Authorities say the property and the owners are still under investigation.

As a family we want this book to help people realise what is going on in this country maybe even in the area you live. We want to help other families like us, find loved ones that have gone missing and whose parents do not know where they are, or whether or not they are still alive. As Darrell's father, I can honestly say that after 8 years, I honestly believed Darrell was dead. His mother on the other hand never gave up and swore to me, "one day I will find him". She was right and for all of us, we are so glad she was right.

My wife has asked me to write a few lines that she hoped would help with the book. So here we go!

I was working on the day that Darrell called to tell his mom he was going on holiday with some friends. When I arrived home that evening, she told me she had reservations about Darrell going with whom he was going but like I told her, Darrell was old enough to make his own mind up and he would be alright.

How wrong was I, we didn't see him again and although 13 years doesn't sound that long in the scheme of one's lifetime, it was.

A week after Darrell went on holiday, he failed to call and see his mom, like he had promised and she was concerned but like I told her, he may have not arrived home until late and maybe he would call the next day. As it was it was someone else who called and told my wife she was Darrell's fiancée, something we later found out was not true. The lady explained to Jean that Darrell had left them and although they had looked for him, they were unable to find him and they had contacted the police.

Jean was quickly on the telephone herself to the police to let them know what had happened and obviously there was now a concern for our son, he could be anywhere. He could be dead! I think it was a couple of days later that the police, who had been unable to find him, asked us about doing an appeal, which we agreed to do. However by the next day, the police had telephoned again to say, that a couple of police officers had made contact with Darrell and had told us, that they had asked him if he was alright and he had said he was. We know, that Darrell will always say that even if he wasn't but because of Darrell's age and because the police had done what is normal "to the book", Darrell was allowed to go on his way. It turns out he had no money; he was trying to get back home, why oh why did he not tell the police that? The reason he wouldn't do that is because Darrell just does what Darrell does.

Now we know Darrell walked for the next two or three days to try to get home but here is where being in the wrong place at the wrong time comes in. Two men stopped Darrell and asked if he wanted some work and although he said no, they knew from talking to him for just a few minutes, here we have a vulnerable person. So they offered him a couple of day's work, so he could earn a little money which would then get him home. Of course they had no intention of that happening and as the story proves, they preyed on his vulnerability.

We had a telephone call; my wife answered but quickly gave the telephone to me. On the other end of the telephone was Darrell. "Dad, I am with two men, who want to give me some work and I want to make a new life for myself here." After discussing why he wanted to make a new life for himself and even telling him, I would come and bring him home, he was adamant, he wanted this new life. The two gentlemen, I hate using that word but at the time that was how I saw them, told me, they would look after him. They said the people he had been on holiday with had been knocking him about and they would make sure he was alright. At this time, I believed them; I had no reason not to. They gave me their mobile telephone number and told me, I could get in touch with Darrell any time we wanted to. So for the next year we spoke with Darrell two or three times but at this time, I had a terrible feeling that Darrell was being told what to say to us. I was scared and had to be careful with what I said because there could be some repercussions to Darrell.

Obviously the police were told of our concerns but unfortunately throughout the whole time Darrell was missing, the police, missing persons, and other charity organisations, would tell us he was a missing contact and not a vulnerable missing person, like we told them. Over time I now know, it is in the police force's interest, as a missing contact causes them a lot less hassle and a lot less money. I cannot talk too much about how my wife and I were unimpressed with their help as there is at this moment an IPCC investigation into how the police dealt with this case.

We did have some contact with Darrell between the years 2000 and 2008, just the odd telephone call. He told us where he was working, Ireland, motorways, farms and other places but each telephone call made me suspect even more that he was being held against his will and being told what to say by someone standing by him listening in to Darrell's calls home. I now know that this is the process these people have of nurturing vulnerable persons into making them think they are looking after them and those (the perpetrators) are their friends.

One of the calls Darrell told us he was married with a baby, (blimey that was quick), we had never even heard he had a girlfriend or a wife and that they were to be proud parents of a child. Most of the few calls we received did not make any sense and I often caught him out with questions, I asked him. I knew he was lying and Darrell never used to be a liar. Of course the police thought my wife and I were paranoid and although they used to come and sit with us sometimes up to three hours, they would always let us down. We begged them, we tried to do their job for them but the overriding factor in all of this was the initial telephone call from Darrell where the two men had told him to say that he wanted to make a new life for himself. They know what to say and do and unfortunately our police force has never taken them seriously. I think from what I have been told both by Gwent Police and the IPCC investigators, they do now, which hopefully might help other vulnerable people in these situations in the future.

The exploitation of human beings, whether they are vulnerable, down on their luck, homeless or whatever category they find themselves in are sought by people similar to who found Darrell. He told us within a few months of being home that the two men who picked him up are responsible within their family for finding people like Darrell, to work for hardly any money or in Darrell's case with no money at all. They exploit these people but make them feel they are their friends. Personally I do not understand the phrase "Stockholm syndrome" but that is what happens, people like Darrell are reduced to feeling less good about themselves and find solace in the fact that the people are exploiting them are in fact family.

Darrell was in a terrible state when we found him, his health was awful, in fact I said if we had not found him when we did, he would not have lasted another six months. Of course I have no proof of that but he looked an old man, more like a hundred years old than the 43 year old man he was.

It was only when we got Darrell home did we realise the extremity of how bad this was. What had happened on that farm wasn't clear, Darrell didn't want to talk to us about it. A few weeks after he came home, the Gwent Police were at our house asking my wife what she wanted done to the people who had done this to Darrell. She told them she wanted them locked up. Of course the police then told us that we could not talk to Darrell about what went on at the farm, so it was difficult for us. We wanted to ask him so many questions!

Of course we did as we were told, that is how we were both brought up and now it was agreed that the police would build a case against the perpetrators and we would help them as much as we could by doing everything they asked of us. The Gwent police were very sympathetic and helped us throughout the time from when Darrell came home to when the court case began. It was very difficult for us all and it almost split our family in two. I was the worst effected and had to have regular meetings with victim support. There came a time when I was suicidal but thankfully, thanks to a lot of people I overcame the problems that all of this turmoil brought us all.

Between the year 2000 and the last time we heard from Darrell, Christmas Eve 2008, my wife never stopped in her search for Darrell. Yes we had holidays and day trips but almost every night Jean was on the computer researching and contacting people to try to help us. We had been to the police as mentioned earlier and they would not help. Missing Persons, Salvation Army, and others were sent e-mails from Jean, begging for help, pleading to find our son. With hindsight, it now makes me smile how, when someone can beg and pray as much as we did and these people in high places can ignore you, it makes no sense. I thought these people were there to help! The only way they came across to me was that they thought we were paranoid.

Jean is an inspiration to anyone else that may be in the same place as we once were. She did more than anyone could have expected, Darrell will never know how much he owes his mom. I find it difficult to understand how even now he takes her for granted but like the police say, he has had his mindset changed over those horrible thirteen years.

After we came back from our holidays Christmas 2008, we expected to hear from Darrell, he had promised to ring us in the New Year. He didn't and now we were starting to feel very worried and again the police were informed of the telephone call on Christmas Eve.

Someone came to the house and spent over three hours taking yet another statement.

I have to talk now about home: during those first 8 years when we had the occasional contact with Darrell it was alright, everyone was playing their part looking for him and even though it was hell we coped very well. Unfortunately after Xmas Eve 2008 and the telephone calls and contact were lost, everything became intolerable.

It was a few years later when I thought that maybe Darrell was dead and my reason for thinking that was that I thought no son of mine would not telephone his mom, he would find a way. Obviously and thankfully I was wrong but I had spoken with our children and told them but I think, although they never said, they agreed with Jean that we would indeed find him.

The longer time went by Jean became more and more obsessed with finding Darrell. I could see how much it meant to her and tried very hard to be supportive and be in the background while she worked away, day and night on the computer, doing everything she could to find a lead. Jean emailed lots of different people most of whom ignored her, those people were usually people in parliament or places where you would have expected some help but it wasn't to be.

I cannot get out of my head how much time Jean actually put in to finding Darrell. Of course a mother is very different to a father but I have to admit, I was beginning to feel like I was less loved by my wife and I noticed the other three children also had concerns about how their mom did not have so much time for them. It wasn't a personal slur, that Jean was doing it on purpose, I don't think she realised. Different people were telling her how impressed they were of her efforts and I think this galvanised her.

Anyhow we coped and at least now we have her back, to being the best mom and the most brilliant wife in the world.

Darrell will never know what his mom and to a lesser degree what the rest of us went through in those thirteen years but I hope when and if he reads this book he will have at least some idea.

There will be an illustration of how important Facebook became in helping us to find Darrell but I at that time was not a Facebook fan and did not get involved. I am sure Jean will explain how Facebook did play its part and of course now because of that I now regularly use the platform myself.

I will now try to explain the two days before we actually were reunited with Darrell. I was watching TV and the telephone rang, Jean usually answered as nine times out of ten it would be for her anyhow. I think I am correct in saying it was a Tuesday evening. Jean took the telephone into the kitchen, she did that often. A few minutes after answering the call she started to cry. There was nothing unusual in that and I expected it was another dead end from a link trying to find Darrell. This was a regular event so at that point I was not unduly worried.

When Jean hung up and came into the lounge she said in a trembling voice that was a lady who thinks she knows where Darrell is. This was the first really concrete piece of information we had had ever. The week before this call, I was told by Jean that someone from the Welsh Echo was going to run a story about Darrell. The story was going to go in the paper the night before, so I readily thought that this may be genuine. The lady had explained roughly whereabouts in Peterstone, South Wales where we might locate him.

I was up and my coat was on and I assumed we would be on our way but Jean put a spanner in the works and said she wanted to telephone Duncan first. The result of that call was that we should not go down at that time of night, but my argument was that we should not wait because anyone holding him against his will - which I had always suspected - would move him if they had read the story in the paper. Duncan wanted to come with us but could not go the next day as he was on a training course at work. This is not what I wanted, I wanted to see if this was a genuine lead and time was of the essence. I still think it was wrong to wait but of course it did not make any difference. If this was to happen to anyone else though in the future, I would hope they would act quicker than we did. Duncan explained to me over the telephone that he would come with Jean and me on Thursday morning and for me to add him to my insurance. I could not sleep that night it was the longest night in history. I was scared, I was hopeful, I was trembling with excitement, and I was not sure whether waiting until Thursday was going to be the cleverest decision I had ever agreed to.

On the Thursday morning we left early, well early for me, I am not an early morning person. Duncan even stopped for a coffee on the way down. I was nervous of what might happen. When we arrived at the location, Duncan pulled over and got out of the car. He walked to a house opposite where we had parked; I was in the back seat, trembling. Duncan was away only a few minutes, probably two or three. When he came back to the car, he said "Darrell is in there, he did not recognise me. Take the car up the road and park and telephone the police, I will wait here.". I argued for a minute or two but he told me it might kick off. We did as we were told and Jean was on the mobile to the police. That proved to be a bit of a problem as Jean was raising her voice and getting stressed with all the stupid questions they were asking her. I had by now parked the car and got out for some fresh air. Jean was still talking with the police but not really getting anywhere, it was a bit of a nightmare to be honest. If someone needs the police urgently why can't they come without all these stupid questions?

It seemed to me like we had been there for what appeared to be twenty minutes or more, Duncan had walked back to the car and it was at this point that I said to Duncan, "Come on mate, let's go and get him." Duncan nodded to me and we started to walk back down to the farm. It was about one hundred and fifty yards away from where we were. I was scared, I have to admit and normally I am scared by nothing. Just as we made it to the driveway, the police arrived. One police officer who had come in a 4 x 4 told me to stay where I was. I said I am going to get my son and he said it could kick off and I was to stay where I was. A riot van arrived within a minute of the other officers arriving and it was at this point I thought this is more serious than I thought.

I could see some comings and goings and I could see police talking with people but I could not see Darrell, although the man that the police had been talking with suddenly started walking towards me. In my head, I believed it was not Darrell because first of all the man walking towards me was hunched and looked too old for it to be him. It was him though and when he got close enough I just hugged him, trembling with all sorts of emotions, disgusted at the smell and embarrassed at his appearance. Unshaven and in disgusting clothes which were ripped torn and had seen better days, I asked him what he had done with himself. His answer was, "I am OK, they look after me they give me stuff." I could not take in what he was telling me, it was like he was happy to be the way he was. I still even to this day, fail to understand this 'Stockholm Syndrome'.

We as a family made a lot of mistakes at the farm so did the police, I don't think any of us realised the seriousness of what had gone on here. Personally, I believed that if these men were the two men who had offered Darrell a new life then why did he look so ill? We were all walking around talking, Jean was very agitated and Duncan told her to calm down. He was afraid that it could kick off but why? There were armed police there to make sure that did not happen.

Jean thankfully took some photographs which was very helpful later as the police had not done so. When it came that there would be a court case those pictures were so important. In my opinion there would have been no court case without those photographs, so well done to Jean for using her motherly instinct on that eventful day.

I can remember Darrell actually asked the man known as little Dan, if it was alright for him to come home with his mom and dad. At the time I thought what is he on about but later, when this Stockholm syndrome was explained to me, I could understand why. They are his masters and he has to obey! He had become accustomed to doing what they told him and his reward was to have food, tobacco and somewhere to put his head down, even if it was a rat-infested shed. Darrell could see nothing wrong with this and over the years accepted that this was his life. I have tried to understand why he could not just get up and walk away but I am told vulnerable people who cannot stand up for themselves have no choice. As a dad, I believe that anyone can just walk away but obviously every human being is different and Darrell as it has been proved does not do anything to get on the bad side of anyone. His captors would have known this and used it to their advantage.

On the way home from the farm, Duncan was driving and Darrell was in the front with him, Jean and I sat in the back. The stench was horrible, I felt sick all the way home. Obviously we were asking Darrell some basic simple questions but he did not appear to really want to answer any of them. He did say that when we asked why he had stopped getting in touch, it was because they had told him we were dead. He has never elaborated on that and because of the police asking us not to interrogate him once it was decided it would go to court we stopped asking him about anything. In fact even though we could now ask him more about his years on that farm, we have not done so and the reason for that was that I said I think we should all move forward rather than looking back. I think that is the right call as there is nothing to gain now with how much pain he suffered. I am sure if I were he, I would not wat to tell my parents of my suffering, it would only make them sad and even though Darrell has been through a terrible ordeal, I am sure he coped with it the best he could and I am equally convinced he doesn't want us to know everything that happened.

When we arrived home, it was perfectly clear Darrell needed a good soak in a bath but unfortunately because of my accident, we only have a walk in shower. We explained to Darrell he needed a good shower and Duncan had already told him he would go home and bring him some clothes as Darrell did not have any. While Darrell was in the shower, I thought to myself, even though he is a man, I needed to check him over. I knocked on the door and told him when you are finished give me a shout and I will come and check how you look. I knew from looking at him when we first set eyes on him he was malnourished but what I was about to find left me speechless. He called me into the bathroom and I said, "Darrell I am sorry to be doing this but I need to check you over," he was wrapped in his towel but he said, "It is alright Dad".

I noticed straight away a massive lump down below it was as big as a size 3 football. I wasn't sure what the hell it was but I knew it was a massive problem. I looked him over and there were cysts, cuts, abrasions, and other minor things that were wrong. I said to him, dry yourself off and I will come into the bedroom and check your feet. His feet were of concern because the trainers he wore on the way home were in a terrible state, soaking wet, torn and really only for the bin. I went into the lounge and told Jean she really needed an urgent appointment at the doctors or the hospital. She was on the telephone when I went back to Darrell trying to sort something out. When I checked Darrell's feet it was obvious he required urgent treatment to them, they were awful, I really do not know how he managed to walk on them.

Jean had arranged an appointment with the doctor and I took Darrell straight away. I have to say at this point I could not understand why the police had not dealt with this on our behalf. I understand now that this is done to anyone that is found in similar circumstances, they are taken to safe houses, checked over by doctors and properly looked after. I think they ignored us because they did not understand what they were dealing with. They let us down badly but maybe this was an isolated case and they did not understand fully how to deal with it, who knows.

When I spoke with the doctor and explained to him why Darrell was in the state he was, the doctor looked at me as though he did not believe me. I was in a state of shock at how Darrell was but the doctor appeared to brush me aside as if I was telling lies about the whole situation. He checked Darrell over in his own sort of way and came to a conclusion that his lump was maybe a hernia. I was later told by a surgeon that doctors are able to ascertain a hernia by shining a light on the lump. This hadn't been done so maybe another case of us being either unlucky or not taken seriously.

We arrived back home from the surgery and I explained to my wife what had just happened and that I wasn't happy and that I would be taking Darrell back to the doctors the next morning to see someone else. I did go the next morning and again I was speechless at how the doctor wasn't taking this situation seriously. It was a case of, well he has some terrible things wrong with him but the process takes time and you will have to wait. Wait we did and I have to make a point of saying that without my wife playing up and I mean playing up, it would have taken more than the **4 months** it took to have the hernia removed than it would have done had we waited for the NHS to react to our terrible situation.

On the Saturday morning Darrell told us he had had a terrible night with the toothache, so off to the hospital for an emergency appointment. We waited patiently, although I was fuming with how the process was being dealt with. I expect this in some countries but not in England. Darrell said he wanted to go in on his own. I didn't think it was a good idea, but look, Darrell was 43 years old and I had to look at the situation from both sides. He was in the room one minute only. I asked what had happened he said, he told the doctor his teeth had been hurting terrible in the night. The doctor said are they hurting now and Darrell said, not so badly. The doctor said come back if they get any worse.

I wasn't very happy, so I arrived home and asked Jean if she could get onto the National Health Service help line to try to get Darrell a top to toe medical. She did and we later found out that this telephone call cost us £9.48, which at the time disgusted me. Here we were trying our hardest to try and pick up the pieces of how someone had so badly treated our son, a son who could not take care of himself like normal people do. Anyhow, my wife managed to get an appointment at Kidderminster Hospital the following day, the Sunday. I was ill that evening as the stress of the last four days had caught up with me, so our youngest son Duncan went with his mom.

They were away a long time, I was beginning to get worried. When they arrived home they told me what had happened and although it was Duncan who went in with Darrell because of the examinations it was both a horrible and embarrassing experience for both Jean and Duncan.

I have a copy of the examination here by my side, I would like to copy some of the documentation:

Consulting Doctor: Henry Obi.

Consultation Details History: Unwell, Fever, Chills and Rigors.

Swelling Right Groin, Poor Feet, Sore Throat and Back Pain.

Examination: Chronically ill-looking. Marked Kyphosis of the thoracic spine, with chest wall deformity.

There is what appears to be an epidermoid cyst on the back. Mouth: poor oral hygiene with several carious teeth both top and lower rows. Gingival hyperplasia pale and anicteric. Chest: Reduced air entry but no crackles. Abdi Giant Right Hernia with?? Hydrocele. Right Hip Severe Restriction in internal rotation sec to ORIF. Left hip some mild restriction, in exterior rotation.

Feet: Severe Onychogryphosis, Tinea Unguim, soles of feet callosity.

Left Leg: Erythema ab igne.

Diagnosis:

Suspected Chest Infection.

Poor Dental Hygiene carious teeth.

Malnutrition.

Inspected Osteoporosis.

Secondary OA Right Hip.

His temperature was 39.6 and his pulse was 77. He was given Amoxicillin Capsules 500mg.

As you can see from the above there were a list of problems that required in my opinion an urgent response but this did not happen and my wife had to fight and fight to get things done. How she wasn't ill over this still baffles me.

In fact in the months to follow, I was convinced that she would have a nervous breakdown, she didn't but it just proves that women are a lot stronger than men and she proved this as it was me that struggled to come to terms with what was to come.

Within a month or so of Darrell being home I started to struggle to come to terms with now sharing a home with my son, a son that I didn't really know. I know that sounds almost impossible to believe but I can tell you, my life as I knew it once all of our children had left home was perfect. I lived with my wife the lady that I married 44 years before and we had a fantastic family life with our children and grandchildren. Yes my wife spent almost every minute of every day trying to find Darrell and yes at times it disturbed me but now at last we have Darrell home and everything should have been more perfect.

It wasn't though, Darrell had gypsy traits and by that I mean he didn't appear to have much respect for him mom or me. I wasn't concerned really about myself but I was concerned how he just sat around enjoying his mom wait on him hand and foot. I spoke with him about it but it didn't register, he didn't appear to care what I said. It went from bad to worse, all he wanted to do was allow his mom to cook, clean, iron, wash his clothes and generally wait on him every day. Yes he had health problems and it appeared he was visiting someone or somewhere every day. I was constantly travelling here there and everywhere and my normal life had gone.

Eventually someone suggested I see a victim support counsellor. At first I wasn't keen as I believe I am quite level headed. It turned out I really did need help. I met up with a lady called Fiona Willetts who just sat and listened to my story. She didn't say much on that first visit and when I left I did think that maybe it was a bit of a waste of time. I was wrong though as later visits proved; Fiona really did make me see things very differently. I always thought that I really do try to look at any problems from different angles but Fiona made me realise a problem shared is a problem solved. I used to say, "Why does Darrell do this or that?" She used to say, "Because he can." How true, all of a sudden, he is able to make choices he hasn't been able to do before and I suppose Darrell loved every minute of it.

My wife and I fell out many times over Darrell's attitude and I was suicidal and on two separate occasions, I really was so close to ending my life. I couldn't cope, even with Fiona's help and it was a real struggle. My wife quite rightly was putting Darrell first and it wasn't something that I had ever known (or liked). Jean has been a terrific mom, grandmother and an even better wife and all of a sudden I was second best. I realised where she was coming from but I couldn't deal with it. No one from any authorities was helping us, we were overcrowded in our home and no one appeared to care.

Having to live with Darrell, who was only interested in horses or sport as an alternative, was difficult. He was very very ill but it didn't appear to bother him. He went with his mom to dentists, doctors, hospitals, to have his feet sorted and probably other places I have forgotten, he never complained.

However all he talked about was horses. I love a bet myself and I love a day out at the races when and if I can afford to go but this constant talking about horses was driving me mad. I would have ITV on the TV and I would pop out to feed my fish. I would come back in and Darrell had turned the TV over to the attheraces channel. Watching rubbish, it drove me mad.

I would go to see Fiona quite regularly at first and through the meetings I became aware that Fiona and others like her did this job voluntarily. I was amazed at how it helped me personally; I became to understand a different way of looking at how Darrell functioned from day to day. It wasn't like there was a magic potion that made everything right but it helped. I wasn't quite so frustrated with Darrell so much. What was happening now though was that Darrell had been living with us for over nine months and we had been begging the authorities for some help with finding Darrell somewhere to live. My wife and I have a two bedroom house and we had a bedroom each until Darrell came home. Now we were sharing a bed again and although it was a way of us chatting together in private, it was difficult as I don't sleep much and am in and out of bed and Jean was getting hardly any sleep. We needed help to find Darrell somewhere to live but the council were awful, they didn't care.

Time moved on and on two occasions, I tried to end it all, unfortunately, each time it happened the one person in my life I could always rely on, my youngest son Duncan, was there to tidy everything up. On the final time however, I think it even got to him and he said he was walking away from everything and leaving us to sort our own lives out. Family relationships were being put into turmoil and it was a combination of so many things that was going on. We had found our son after all these years but were now faced with very little help from the authorities and loads of problems to solve. I am ill, I have bad health but I was being asked to do this do that, come here go there, daily, I had no life.

There was a court case pending, we had a date, we thought, if we can get past this, and then surely there would be life at the end of the tunnel. Of course what happened next shouldn't really happen but it did. The judge was going on holiday to America, so the date of the trial had to be put back. It could only happen to us. The trial had been set for March of 2014 and then it was finally given as September 2014, only 6 months and everyone was surprised at how much it affected us.

Finally the trial day arrived and it was horrible. Darrell was scared he would bump into his captors at the court. Jean and I were going to have to go to Cardiff with Darrell purely as support for the four days Darrell was to give evidence. We were not allowed in the court and the Gwent Police made sure Darrell was picked up each morning and brought back to the hotel after the day's process had been finished. They were a godsend, in relation to looking after us all. One of the police officers that were put on the case to look after us, DC Paul Cole had been to our house many times to keep us informed of what we had to do in relation to the trial. He talked us through what we could do and what we could not do and although my wife especially and me not so much, had no time for the police because of the way the police had failed to help us in terms of trying to find our son, Mr Cole helped us to begin to trust the police again.

The trial was difficult, not for me personally because like my dad used to say, if you tell the truth no harm can come to you. Unfortunately during and after the trial, it is plain to see that both sides are not equal. The guilty party DO tell lies. I won't go into the ins and outs of the trial as I am sure my wife will cover that, as like she said, the people responsible did not get punished nowhere near as much as they should have been, mainly because of the stupid law in this country. A law, which I think is now being brought up to date and which hopefully will support people like us in the future.

The son was given four and a half years, which I hope is killing him on a daily basis, like us not having Darrell around for thirteen years, killed us. I hope he has a conscience although having met him, I doubt that very much. After the trial, our lives became more tolerable and slowly but surely we began to get our lives back on track.

Just before the trial date, Darrell had been given keys to his new home, it was August 4th 2014, just a matter of 17 months after him arriving at our door. I just wonder if all the refugees arriving on these shores had to wait 17 months for some living accommodation, would they stay or would they go home. Maybe our government should try it.

Darrell's mom and I had to refit his home with everything, as obviously it was unfurnished but with the help of family and friends we did it and Darrell finally had a home he could call his own. He tries to keep it clean and does OK but without his mom he would not cope. He still even now does not understand the value of money but why should he, he didn't handle any for 13 years. We have all of his direct debits set up, so he cannot get into any financial problems. We are helping the best we can, trying to teach him to cook and do menial tasks but Darrell finds it difficult.

He has recently been found to be on the autistic range, something his mom has had to fight for, for almost 2 years. After being assessed Darrell was found to be autistic, have behaviour problems and mild learning difficulties. The assessment will hopefully enable us to understand Darrell more as we have found it difficult at times. If everything is structured in his life he is content but if anything happens that disrupts that he sulks and becomes difficult. We await someone somewhere to help us with that but again we won't hold our breath.

Darrell has made some strides forward, he has his own home, which he keeps adequately clean. His mom keeps on top of him as Darrell's idea of clean to ours is very different. We have to remember though that for 13 years no one ever complained to him about the way he dressed or washed or kept his living accommodation clean. Remember he lived in squalid conditions and in his head it was alright to look like he did and be as he was.

There is a big difference in his appearance now and probably because of that he has found himself a girlfriend. Last week he went on a four day break with her to Newquay, where according to Sue (his girlfriend's name), he was a perfect gentleman.

Jean and I want the best we can get for Darrell, we think he deserves that. It has been a very difficult road for all of the family and at times, I personally could never imagine life for him as it is now. He still likes his bet on the horses but he isn't as bad as he was. He is slowly beginning to understand the cost of living and the consequences of having no money. It is fair to say that although Darrell does voluntary work at the moment, he is looking forward to getting back to work. We don't know when that will be because of his fear of meeting "nasty" people but I am sure in the coming months he will finally make that all important step back into full time work.

I hope I have helped with my version of events and if reading this book helps just one family who has gone through what we have all gone through, then it will have been worth the time I have spent doing this.

Mr A J Simester

Chapter 16

A message from Fiona Willetts, Victim Support – a Volunteer Serious Crime Support Worker

I had, like many others, learned about the atrocities of slavery during my history classes at school. We were told that slavery was abolished in the 19th century; putting an end to people being stolen from their homes to become someone else's property.

But two centuries after the Parliament of the United Kingdom became the first country to abolish slavery, it is still happening in nearly every country of the world – including the UK. The slave traders in my school books operated fairly openly, whereas modern day slavery is secretive. Tragically, people are still being bought and sold, including children, as well as being made to go into bonded and forced labour or early and forced marriages, and are being trafficked from one country to another. When slavery happens on your doorstep, it is all the more shocking – because we think it can't happen here.

I first met with Tony Simester shortly after he had been reunited with his son Darrell, and he was struggling to cope emotionally and practically. Darrell had been missing for 13 years, and his family were desperate to find him. While he was missing, Darrell Simester had been held on a farm in South Wales. A vulnerable man had been a victim of slavery, until being discovered weeks beforehand. He had been held captive in appalling conditions, forced to work for no pay, and beaten regularly until he was found in February 2013.

I was in Victim Support's office in Kidderminster when a Detective Constable asked what we could do to support Tony. As a volunteer with the independent charity, I have had rigorous training to support people who have been the victim of a crime. I agreed to meet with Tony to explain our services and support him. It would be easy to presume that, as Darrell was now home safe, everything would be getting back to 'normal'. While the family were overjoyed to be reunited, they were also feeling overwhelmed by the situation.

At Victim Support, because the charity has supported millions of different victims of crime, we know that it is impossible to pre-empt how a crime may affect an individual or those around them. Instead, I am trained to listen to what is being said, verbally and non-verbally, and work out what support a victim might find useful to their particular circumstances. Tony was no exception.

On my first meeting with Tony, it was apparent that Tony was feeling extremely guilty about much of Darrell's situation, including his learning disability. Tony is a proud family man who has an inherent need to protect his family, and felt that he was failing to do so. Tony was struggling to find ways of coping with everyday life and knew that he was in danger of falling into seriously poor mental health; therefore, it was imperative that, between us, we found some forms of coping mechanisms.

Our minds can sometimes feel overloaded with information, worries and thoughts and it can be very difficult to separate the thoughts. Tony was finding this very hard to deal with, and as a result, he was struggling to get things done as he didn't know where to start. Tony's life was usually ordered and he had a fair amount of routine. After Darrell came home, routine and order were nigh on impossible at that time. Tony had had severe depression following an accident some years before and was concerned that he wouldn't be able to manage his emotions at this time and was unsure of where that would lead. He felt that suicide was a real threat to him. After discussions with Tony, he decided that writings lists may help. This could have been lists of thoughts, solutions or ideas that would help him to cope on a day-to-day basis. I also arranged through Victim Support commissioned services for Tony to have six sessions of immediate counselling.

Tony was also finding it extremely difficult to deal with home life as, although he was overjoyed at having his son home, the family dynamics had changed drastically. It had just been Tony and Jean at home. Their days were spent searching for their son and supporting others who had loved ones who were missing. Tony said that their lives were calm and organised. Tony and Jean enjoyed holidays together and spending time with each other and the family. Darrell was always at the forefront of his mind but he had learnt to cope. Tony felt he had no control over his life anymore and that he had 'lost' his wife, who was understandably overjoyed at having Darrel home and was very protective of him. Around this time, I also spoke to Jean on the telephone, who was also finding it hard to understand Tony's depression and attitude. Not only did they want to spend time getting to know their son again; in the early days of Darrell being home, they also faced a whirlwind of appointments for health visits and statements to the police. Tony was finding it challenging to understand his own thoughts and emotions and therefore impossible to understand the thoughts of the other members of the family.

Being held in captivity against the victim's will, will have a massive negative effect on a person's psychological and physical well-being. Darrell had been held in appalling conditions for so long that he had developed foot rot, as well as many other health conditions that needed urgent treatment. He, like other victims of slavery, was denied health care or any other assistance; for fear that he would speak out and as a way to further control him.

Darrell was diagnosed with a degree of Stockholm syndrome, which is a psychological symptom that a victim can develop when they have been held in captivity. This in itself made it difficult for all involved as Darrell would have felt a degree of empathy towards his captors and possibly felt that he should protect the perpetrators.

Generally, when a victim has had all control taken away from them through crime, they may feel, consciously or sub-consciously, that they need to have full control over their lives. This can be very difficult for family members and friends, as the victim may be seen as being selfish or even as a controlling person themselves.

As Darrell had never been formally diagnosed with a specific learning disability, it was difficult for Tony to comprehend Darrell's understanding of what was expected of him. For example, Tony had said that he had tried to engage Darrell in conversation but often, Darrell's response was simply yes or no answers. Tony felt frustrated and felt that Darrell didn't want to engage with him. Throughout our sessions together, we discussed how Darrell may have felt that this answer was all that was needed and may have needed more open questions instead of closed questions.

Darrell loves all things sporty and more than anything horse racing. After years of slavery, with no option to be out in the community, Darrell could make choices about how he lived his life. This would include betting on horse races every day and going to the local shop to buy nothing but crisps and unhealthy snacks, all things that he couldn't do whilst in captivity.

This was a constant source of worry to Tony, and conflicts between the family ensued. It was apparent that the family were close and full of love for each other, but everyone dealt with their own emotions in different ways. That love and protectiveness of each other helped to resolve their conflicts.

By June 2013, Darrell's benefits had been sorted, and his health was improving, although there were still no formal assessments forthcoming for a diagnosis on Darrell's disabilities. Tony said that, at this point, as we had spent many sessions discussing coping strategies, he was finding things easier at home although he missed spending time alone with Jean.

During the time of the press releases in September 2013, Tony was finding it hard to watch Darrell's and Jean's reaction to the news on TV or in the newspapers. Darrell was visibly upset and Tony was unsure of how to comfort him as the reports were concerning other victims of the same captors too. Tony's priorities were with Darrell and Jean at this time.

Tony's depression had become more severe over the period of March/April 2014. The trial had been postponed until September 2014. In the previous year, I had discussed how Tony and Jean could arrange a needs assessment for Darrell that could help towards his independence. The family had asked for a needs assessment to be carried out for Darrell, and had finally achieved this, only for Darrell to be assessed as having no substantial needs. Darrell was also on a waiting list for housing, but no appropriate properties were forthcoming. Tony saw no end to the situation they were in or any hope for Darrell to live the independent life that he craved. During this time, I had appealed to the police to arrange a multi-agency meeting that I could also attend to help to ensure the best all-round support for Darrell, and the best outcome. I attended meetings with the family and also meetings with Darrell's housing officer and social services (who were yet to allocate a social worker to Darrell), to reiterate how important it was that Darrell's needs were being met.

The family dealt with agencies which they felt were letting them down during and after Darrell's ordeal.

Tony felt that, if he took his own life, his family would find it easier and be much happier. This intense time for Tony lasted for a couple of weeks and was very difficult for the family too. I saw or spoke to Tony constantly over this period of time. Tony had hit rock bottom and decided to leave the family home. I called Tony and Jean regularly to check on his welfare. Tony returned home after a short period and Darrell moved into temporary accommodation. Darrell had a property allocated to him in August 2014, finally gaining his independence and is now doing well. It took more than a year for the family to feel that things may be moving in the right direction for their son in terms of his independence.

Of course, the trial was at the forefront of everyone's mind. The police and Crown Prosecution Service find gathering evidence in a case of slavery or trafficking extremely difficult. And it is hard for us, as volunteers supporting crime victims, because we cannot discuss evidence with them. Quite often, victims want to discuss everything in lots of detail, to hopefully answer unanswered questions.

Victims who have been held over a period of time may be confused over dates and details. In order to cope daily while in captivity, they may have learned dissociation, where a victim may have blocked out events from their minds. They may be disorientated or anxious. There may be memory loss or lapses, or varying degrees of Stockholm syndrome.

Threats, violence, or forcing a victim to witness the violence or even death of another person may be used to show the consequence of going against a captor's wishes. Darrell was led to believe that there was a body of another victim of slavery buried in a nearby field, reinforcing to Darrell that it could possibly happen to him. Darrell was coerced into working long days for no pay, and his vulnerability was used in order to achieve this. Darrell has since been diagnosed with Autistic Spectrum condition, with associated learning disabilities. Darrell has difficulties in social interaction, social communication and social imagination. Darrell's captors had used this to their advantage. Darrell found it easier to have no social expectations of him and routines were kept to a minimum within the compounds of the farm. Darrell couldn't make any decisions while in captivity, as that right was taken away from him. By the time that Darrell returned home, the ability to make basic decisions was extremely difficult. Darrell had to be reminded of basic hygiene tasks, safety precautions and social skills that had been 'unlearned' while he was held as a slave. This was extremely exhausting for Tony, as at that time, Darrell's Autism was undiagnosed and he couldn't understand why Darrell was acting this way. We discussed this on many occasions to find a way of helping Tony to see the situation from a different perspective.

Darrel gave 3 days of evidence at the trial and the rest of the family gave their evidence. Tony said he was not worried about giving evidence as quite early in my support, we had discussed the court procedures, and how he could answer questions with simple answers and simply tell the truth. Tony said that he kept this in mind and most of the time during the trial was coping well, however, there were also times on hearing evidence that he felt extremely angry. Jean was very ill during the trial, which made the already traumatic experience even harder. Whilst one of the accused had his charges dropped after a plea bargain, the other was sentenced to four and a half years in prison. This is less than a third of the time that Darrell was kept captive by him.

Darrell was left with, not just emotional scars, but also physical scars, which may be a constant reminder of the atrocities that he has had to endure. Poor nutrition has led to ongoing health issues. Darrell has had to endure operations and many trips to dentists and GPs. The Simester family are unsure of how large the family or gang of people who may be involved with the captors who held Darrell and one of the fears for them is reprisals from members that may not have been caught. This has led to a mistrust of people and worries about other's motives, anxieties and isolation. The whole family feel an inherent need to protect Darrell from further abuses and have ultimately drawn a balance between protecting him and allowing him his independence, which goes to show how much of a strong bond the family unit have.

Barriers were present that stopped Darrell from escaping, for example, fear, financial, a willingness to please, and empathy with his captors. Darrell also has a special interest, as is usual with individuals who have Autistic Spectrum Condition. He loves horses, which he worked tirelessly to look after at the farm. There would have been many reasons for Darrell to feel that he had to stay where he was.

Although I initially supported Tony, over a period of time I became involved with Jean and Darrell too. The support that was given was primarily was allowing Tony to have someone to talk to in a non-judgmental, confidential manner. I also provided practical support, for example, referring Tony for counselling sessions and being involved with multi-agency meetings and other meetings with professionals, contacting the police for updates, making sure that Darrell's and the family's needs were being met.

No two victims have the same needs as each person will react differently and have a different history, coping strategies and preferences. It is important that the right support is offered as soon as possible; although, often this may be refused primarily, as the victim may feel ashamed or feel that they want to just forget the experience. Support can be from a number of different agencies depending on the needs of the victim. For example, housing, police, welfare and benefits agencies, schools, health care and organisations offering emotional and practical support.

About Victim Support

Victim Support started as a local victim support scheme in Bristol and was the idea of a social work lecturer, Chris Holtom, and a worker at a charity called NACRO, Nigel Whiskin, when they realised that victims of crime had very little support. Over the years, more areas adopted the scheme, until nowadays; Victim Support is an independent national charity who has helped over 25 million victims and witnesses and is the oldest and largest victim's charity in the world.

Victim Support offers free help to victims of any crime, or those affected by a crime against someone they know, irrespective of whether the crime has been reported to the police and regardless of when it happened.

Victim Support helps victims and some witnesses to 'Find the Strength' to move on after crime, by offering emotional support with an opportunity to be listened to, in a non-judgemental manner. Most of the support is given by volunteers, who offer choices and information to help a victim regain control over their lives. They can also help a victim to make sense of what they have been through.

Victim Support also offers practical help. Often a victim will struggle with practical issues, as the focus is on coping emotionally. Victim Support can help with filling out forms, for example, insurance claims or compensation claims, or completing Victim Personal Statements. They can also help with applying to be rehoused, arranging medical treatment or helping to understand the criminal justice system. Victim Support may recognise that other agencies may be able to help and they can arrange for referrals to the appropriate agency.

Victim Support offers specialist services alongside of the main services. These include hate crime, antisocial behaviour, sexual violence and domestic violence. Also provided are opportunities for restorative justice and support for young victims and witnesses.

I am proud to be a part of Victim Support, with such clear values and purpose.

Our Purpose

Our purpose is to help people find the strength to move on after crime.

We give emotional and practical support that is a source of strength and comfort.

We make people feel better.

We use the local understanding of our volunteers and staff to help victims and witnesses take control, so we can all live in a safer and more caring society.

Everything Victim Support does will always be based on empathy and an understanding of victims' and witnesses' needs, so people are mentally and physically better off after we have helped them.

We want to be a force for good in society.

If you have been affected by crime and would like someone to talk to, you can call the Victim Support Supportline on: 08 08 16 89 111 (weeknights between 8pm and 8am, weekends Saturday 5pm to Monday 8am). Or visit www.victimsupport.org.uk for more information or to find details of your local victim care office.

Chapter 17

Clare Hutchinson Newspaper Reporter - BBC Wales TV

I was working as a crime reporter at the South Wales Echo newspaper when Jean and Tony first made contact. My then-editor sent me an email he had received, and asked me to look into it. When I opened the email and saw it was about a missing person, I have to admit my heart sank a little.

As a crime reporter I often received press releases from the police or messages from concerned families asking for help to find their loved ones. Sometimes the missing person would be a confused older person, or someone with mental health issues – and the final outcome would sometimes be tragic. At other times people would contact my paper asking for help to find long-estranged parents, or children, who they had been separated from decades before. Sometimes all they would have is a first name and a vague place – "Does anyone know a David who lived in the Rhondda in the 1950s? He may have been a miner?"

Sometimes I would be able to write stories about these searches, but usually it felt like shouting into the abyss – rarely would anything come of it, perhaps because the person they were looking for did not always want to be found. These were my thoughts when I opened that email from Jean back in early 2013 – but as soon as I began to read it, I realised this was something entirely different.

The long email told the story of a loving, close family - just like yours or mine. Four siblings, two parents, a suburban upbringing, a quiet life. One of their sons, Darrell, had needed more support than the other children. Jean described him in the email as "vulnerable". At the time, I didn't completely understand what she meant: was he diagnosed with a learning difficulty? Did he have drug and alcohol problems? But now, of course, I understand exactly what she means. A loving, kind son who is extremely trusting. Who is - as Jean so succinctly puts it - "easily-led". The email suggested that sometimes Darrell tested his parents' patience, but Jean, Tony and their family all clearly loved him to bits.

Then one August in 2000, Jean wrote, he came to tell her he was going on holiday with another family he was living with at the time. A week later, a woman Jean had never met came to her door to explain that she had been with Darrell on that holiday, and that after an argument he had run away. They hadn't seen him since and in the end had returned home without him.

The Simester family's lives were simply changed forever.

What followed in the email was a long and heartrending account of Jean's. It's a story she and Tony can tell better than I ever could, because I didn't live through it. I can't even imagine the impact it must have had on their lives over 13 long years. At first they heard from their son infrequently, speaking to him in halting phone calls, with voices in the background which seemed to be telling him what to say. Soon the number was withheld and questions about Darrell's location led to further suspicion when he answered: "I'm not allowed to tell you".

Hinted at in the email was the growing, sickening suspicion that Darrell may be being held against his will. Jean told of 13 years of worry and fear; of frequent, frustrated attempts to interest the police and missing person's charities in Darrell's disappearance; of moments of hope and then of dismay when her desperate search was rejected by professionals time and time again. The words she used were so powerful they will forever be etched into my memory: "They told me he was a missing contact. He isn't a missing contact - he's my son."

Equally poignant was that after Darrell's calls stopped, Jean and Tony kept the phone he last reached them on. It was always charged, always switched on, just in case. Finally, Jean explained, they followed the long thread of Darrell's disappearance to Cardiff. A friend helped them trace a mobile phone number used by Darrell in an early phone call to a paving firm in Rumney - a sprawling suburb on the eastern side of Cardiff.

Tony and his sons had already made the long journey to Rumney more than once to try and find Darrell. They had printed off leaflets with his photo and taken it to all the places he may go: the betting shop, the pub - anywhere they could think of. Then on a Facebook page dedicated to the search and followed by people from all over the country, someone suggested trying the local paper.

So here they were.

I spoke to Jean on the phone in February 2013. When I read her email I was already suspicious that something more was going on, that Darrell had not disappeared out of choice. And after speaking to Jean - such a genuine, loving mum who had almost worried herself and her family to collapse over the years - I gave serious thought to the possibility that Darrell may be being held against his will.

I had in recent months written stories relating to trafficking and slavery. Wales is the first country in the UK to have introduced an official in charge of raising awareness of human trafficking and coordinating the work of police and charities to make them better at recognising and helping victims. I had interviewed the first anti-trafficking coordinator and his successor, and had written stories about people who had been rescued and then cared for by a local charity, Bawso.

But when experts told me about trafficking, it was categorised neatly into different types: domestic servitude, sex slavery, forced labour. And almost without exception, the victims were generally thought to be foreign. Perhaps smuggled into the country or around the country. Desperate to come to Britain, they had walked into a horrific trap, and their lack of language skills and knowledge of the country - coupled with sheer fear - had prevented their escape.

Yet here was the son of two lovely people from a town near Kidderminster, how could he possibly be a victim of trafficking?

Of course, we now know the answer to that. While early charges of slavery were dropped, father and son Daniel Doran and David Daniel Doran stood trial for forced labour in 2014. While Daniel Doran was found not guilty, his son David admitted his guilt part-way through the trial and was sentenced to four-and-a-half years. The judge made his thoughts clear when he described Darrell's treatment as "repellent and wrong", and "not much better than a slave".

At the newspaper back in 2013, we suspected some form of trafficking may have occurred, but on legal advice took the decision to print Jean's story as a straightforward search for a missing person. It was published across two pages, with Jean's quotes from her email, a photo of Darrell from his school days, smiling ear-to-ear, and another, grainier, one of him at the time he went missing. It was a last-ditch attempt by two desperate parents after 13 years of searching but – incredibly - it paid off.

I was in work on a rainy morning in late February 2013, a couple of days after the story went to press, when I got a tearful phone call from Jean. I had wondered if the story would come to anything. We had printed both my office number and a mobile phone number used by Tony and Jean at the end of the story, but as time passed I had begun to accept that it may be yet another typical end to a missing person story, with us shouting into the abyss, and no one answering back.

Nothing prepared me for what Jean had to say on that morning: she was so emotional it was hard to properly understand her, but I heard the words: "Someone thinks they know him, he's on a farm, we're on our way there." I hardly had time to scribble down the address. I promised her I would meet them there, and urged them to involve the police.

I drove out to the farm, which was on the Gwent marshes right on the edge of the city, and met Jean, Tony and Darrell's brother Duncan outside Cariad Farm just as the police arrived. A photographer from my newspaper was already there, and he recorded the incredible scenes we all witnessed that day.

I don't think the Simester family had known what to expect – or even whether the man they had been tipped off about would be their son. When I got there Duncan hurriedly told me he had already approached his brother, but when Darrell told him he wasn't allowed to leave the farm the family were concerned enough to call the police.

Then I saw Darrell. He was walking out of the farm and through the white gate pillars towards the road we were on. Hunched over and with his dad by his side, he was wearing torn, filthy clothes, a flat cap and lugging one black bin bag filled - I later discovered - with filthy old clothes. His face was dirty and furrowed with deep lines. He looked exhausted and dazed. In Tony's words, his son looked like an old man.

But it was Darrell's reunion with his mum that left an indelible mark on my memory. Jean ran up and wrapped him in a huge bear hug, and wouldn't let him go. It seemed to be saying, "never again". It was a moment that, as a mother, she must have always hoped for - and I could see she didn't want to ever let him go again.

I later asked Jean what she said to her son at that moment. Her reply was simple: "I just said, you're coming home."

Tony, Jean and Duncan were, I think, in a state of shock. They gathered around the car with Darrell, and it felt incongruous to be laughing and making small talk while Darrell smoked a rolled cigarette and let his mum fuss over him. After finishing his cigarette Darrell and his family simply got in their car and returned home to Kidderminster.

Over the following weeks and months I stayed in contact with Jean, Tony and Duncan, to check on Darrell's progress. We published a story following his discovery, with a beaming photograph of Jean hugging Darrell on the front page. But behind the story of celebration, we knew there could be a far more disturbing tale that may one day be told. Printing that suspicion was out of the question, for legal reasons. But my phone calls with Tony changed it from a suspicion to a near-certainty.

The first shock came for the family when they got home and discovered the terrible condition Darrell was in: a hernia on his groin the size of a football; a fungal infection that had turned the soles of his feet green; curvature of the spine and severe weight-loss.

Darrell would wake up every day at 6am, his dad said. He would fall asleep in the armchair in the evening, but jerk awake at the sound of a person walking into the room, or closing a door. While his parents believe he had learning difficulties from a young age, he was now also suffering deep psychological problems and has since been seeing a psychiatrist.

Slowly the police investigation got underway, taking its time due to the difficulty in balancing Darrell's delicate physical and mental health with the need to find out what happened. Tony and Jean can tell more about that - but for me, it was a question of checking in with the family whenever I could. And while they certainly had an extremely rocky road to tread, for an outsider like me, I could also see the incredible progression they made with their son over such a short period of time.

Together they went on holidays, took day trips to see his favourite football teams, held a homecoming party and – more recently – helped Darrell move into his new place. And those were just some of a thousand little things the family has done to get Darrell's, and their own lives, back on track.

After I joined the BBC, we went to visit Darrell for a programme in which we wanted to tell their story, and he showed us around his new house with pride. There was a clock on the mantelpiece that used to belong to his grandmother; DVDs and books donated by well-wishers; a Manchester United duvet on the spare bed; and a huge pile of neat triangular sandwiches Darrell had made for our arrival.

His family helped him develop routines for cleaning and cooking. When we visited a new kitchen had just been fitted - and Jean was planning to help her son make a cheesecake. Since then Darrell's joined Facebook, and among invitations to join Candy Crush and other games, I've seen a least one photo of a carefully-baked cake.

As Tony said to me after the trial: "I've banned all talk of the last 13 years – we just want to look forward and talk about the years to come."

It's a long road, but the progress the Simester family has already made is incredible. And hopefully their story and their openness to tell it will have a real impact on the lives of others.

Chapter 18

Darrell's Views in His Own Words

This is Darrell's experience in his own words, short and sweet: As he wrote it spelling mistakes and all.

13 Years of Hell.

Part 1. I went to Porthcawl on holiday for a week with some English People and I had a argument with the kids over something and left them in a caravan and left them there and left the caravan park alone.

And on the same day I left I slept in a bus stop one day and moved on the next day and headed for the nearest road to get to the motorway.

On the Sunday Some Policepersons stop their car and Asked if I need help, and I said I wanted to get back to Kidderminster so there said the couldn't help me. So I moved on and I headed too the nearest stop and I stopped at a Palace Newport Town centre and at that time I just had the same clothes on and no money at a time, so I walking the streets in Newport for a couple of Days and headed for the motorway and took the wrong turning and finished up on Taffs Well on the motorway.

And on the same day this red pick up – Lorry stopped and one the lads asked if I wanted any work at the time, and I said I know I just wanted to go back home, and the Driver said come and work for us for a couple of days.

So there took them with them and I Do 2 days work doing block paving for 2 days from Thursday & Friday without pay and one bloke said on A Saturday I'll take you to my father's farm at Carriad Farm.

When I was working for 2 days their put me up in a caravan in a place called Shirenewton Caravan Park.

Part 2. So on Saturday morning this young person came out of his caravan and said to me are you ready to go to the farm and took me too Cariad farm to see what I was doing for the next the years of hell I was going to do. So I got out of the Lorry and meet there family and walked around the yard and got too meet this family and see what I was going too do for the next 13 years of hell.

So I meet this Young Person about 26 and his farther about 60 and asked if I had with horses before and I said know and I said to this young person where am I stopping and showed me a building with a table cups kettle milk couch heated fire and know blankets to keep me warm, so I just had a leather jacket to cover me and clothes to keep warm. I said to one of them what time do I start work and one of them start at 700pm of morning.

So the next day I asked if I could ask for a phone to ring my family. So I borrowed his phone but when I was speaking to my family he was telling me what to say to them.

So into my second week their asked me to go to a farm audition to sell horses the name of this Auction was called Brecon.

So 4 of us left Carriad farm and headed for Brecon and didn't get back too the farm till about 5-6.30 in the evening. So when we got back and unloaded the animals of the Lorry and put them in their sheds, one lad said take the last one of and take too the bottom of the yard and tie it up to the Poll, and when I tied it up this one person told me to get on this 16 hands horse and Jump on it but I didn't know how to ride a horse so this person told me to jump on a wall and put my leg across it back and said too hold it maine and keep my legs so close to its side of the horse body.

One day the young lad asked me to ride a mare and I saddled it up with a bridle with a mare colt and Rode it up the top of the yard when a Sawdust Plastic bag flew out and frightened both of them and Got rid of me and it unshipped me on to the Concrete and I hurt myself.

So all of them rushed up and put me in a wheelbarrow because I couldn't walk down to the bottom of the yard.

I knew at the time I knew I had broken my hip on the right side and it took them 2 days to hospital and use a false name at the hospital. I was in hospital for a week and the next week back to work with crutches.

So for those 13 years I worked on a farm for working 2 meals a day and no pay, but the last 16 months one of them bought a caravan to sleep in. There was know shower for 11 years until the last 2 years, so I had to wash in a basic bowl or horse troff.

Part 3. One day a woman down the road was walking her dog and got in touch with my family and told them where I was working at. So on the Thursday 28th February my family Duncan, Mom and dad found me in a state looking like my Grandad.

On the Day I left I stood by the Lorry and 5 of us was talking together their where myself young Dan a lady and Dad a policeman, and at that time young Dan brought out a wod of money and handed me £40 to me and I thought to myself whats that for, so I left and walked away from the farm and walked between the gates and met my mom outside and had the biggest hug and told me you'll coming home with us, and at that time their was a photo person outside wanted too take a few photo of myself and mom together.

So the 4 of us jumped into the car and went back home to Kidderminster.

Part 4. So when I got home Duncan went home and brought me a bag of clothes for me too wear, so I walked into a shower and Dad told me when I have finished he told me to shout him, so I has a shower and dried myself off and walked into a small bedroom and I shouted to my Dad and said I finished so he walked into the bedroom and said what is that hanging between my legs and I told him it was a hernia.

So mom got in touch with the hospital to get a appointment for it and get appointment for my feet. I had my hernia done on 28th June 2014 and my feet done as well so on 4 weeks in I had a bloke come to the house and took photos of me all over my body.

And few weeks down the line 2 wales police person came down and told me to do a interview live in Kidderminster for 5/6 days to tell the story of the last 13 years. So I done those interviews for them and at that time doing those interviews there was myself Paul Cole asking questions and Moira sat next to me if I was struggling any questions to answer.

So on 23rd September 2014 Myself mom and Dad had too do their trail in front of their family, but I had too do my live interview in a separate room and so I didn't have to see the accused person standing in court. I done my interview for 4 days and Mom done hers for half hour.

So on 24/ 25/26/27 September 2014 and Mom and Duncan did theirs on Mondays 29th September and Dad done his on 3rd October and the live sentenced was 24th October and Dan was GUILTY on 8th October and he got 2 half years instead of 5 years in jail.

The Court Case was the Worst place to be in because their family was sitting on the right of court and the Simester and Police and friends was sat on the left side.

And when young Dan walked into the court and turned around and see his family and smiled back to them. And when the Judge told him he was getting 2 half years in jail, I wished he had got 5-10 years in prison.

Part 5. I would like to thank everybody who's has been in touch with our family, their included.

The Police from Wales Gwent Police

The Police from Kidderminster

Clare Hutchinson from BBC Wales

Vulnerable adult Police Station

Chapter 19

Duncan Simester

This is from Darrell's brother Duncan:

Darrell my brother, who I would do anything for, the same
goes for the rest of my family, I'm that guy
Who would take a bullet for anyone of them, that's just the
way I'm made. But in life there are things that
are out of our control like taking someone's hurt and making
it go away, something that I wish over the
last few years I could have done, .my parents have been to
hell and back many many times with it
Getting to the stage where they have both tried to take their
own lives. As a loving son how am I
Supposed to cope with this? I've cried myself to sleep on
many occasion wishing that I could stop their
Hurt I want to be as honest as I can be and it might upset
some people but I've always spoken how I've
Found so that's why I'm writing this for the book as much as
finding Darrell and getting him home and

now to see how well he is doing was it the best thing we did
and honestly I don't know I can't answer
that I really wish I could, you have to be in our situation to
totally understand where I'm coming from I
think, does all the pain that mom and dad have gone through
justify it I don't think so yes I know how
much hurt they were going through before but what has
shocked me is the pain that makes you so low
you want to take your own lives after they have found the one
thing that they have been looking for for
the past 13 years so do you see my point? Was it all worth it?
Because at the time this was unheard of
trying to get support from people was a waste of time nobody
could understand what had happened
and friends would ask questions about why Darrell had been
missing for so long and why he hadn't
been found earlier, you would try to answer there question
and they would shake their heads you want
to try living our lives I'd think to myself we can't get our
head round it and for us it 24/7 you brain never
switches off, it like a time bomb waiting to go boom. I was
able to drive home and take a breather mom
and dad couldn't, my parent went through hell not knowing
for 13 years where Darrell was imagine that
then on 28 February 2013 we found him all the hard work had
paid off NO the hard work started that
day and still to this day they are still working hard to help
Darrell we as siblings shake our heads at
what they still do for him they should be enjoying retirement
but they are always running around for
him this is unfair he has to stand on his own two feet more
and this annoys me massively do you see
where I'm coming from with this people while he was
missing they had a life and now they don't. Darrell
can look after himself yes I know he is not the smartest but
he's a survivor and must be allowed to grow

up on his own which we hope he will do mom and dad I love
you to bits but let him grow I understand
that you want to watch over him and protect him but he needs
to find himself I would like to personally
thank every single one of you that helped in getting my
brother back home and all the people who helped in
his recovery. I hope that other families that go through
anything similar are helped like we were and
people learn from this case... to anyone who wants to hurt my
family in any way come see
me.

Duncan Simester

At the time of the book going to be published, I am in
contact with Kevin Hyland OBE MP Independent
Commissioner For Anti-Slavery, who has promised to help.
He is coming to visit us.

To finalise:

Everyone who has contributed to this book, hope and pray
that it will help others in the future. What we experienced
should never have happened. If we can stop families in the
future not having to live through what we did, then this will
be all worthwhile.

Darrell Now (2015)

16400629R00071

Printed in Great Britain
by Amazon